Resilience

Memoir of a Broken Little Girl

Becoming a Woman of
Strength and Beauty

TONI LONTIS

First published by Ultimate World Publishing 2018

Copyright © 2018 Toni Lontis.

ISBN

Print: 978-1-925884-07-4

Ebook: 978-1-925884-06-7

Toni Lontis has asserted her right under the Copyright, Designs and Patents Act 1988 to be identified as the author of this work. The information in this book is based on the author's experiences and opinions. The publisher specifically disclaims responsibility for any adverse consequences, which may result from use of the information contained herein. Permission to use information has been sought by the author. Any breaches will be rectified in further editions of the book.

All rights reserved. No part of this publication may be reproduced, stored in or introduced into a retrieval system, or transmitted in any form, or by any means (electronic, mechanical, photocopying, recording or otherwise) without the prior written permission of the author. Any person who does any unauthorised act in relation to this publication may be liable to criminal prosecution and civil claims for damages. Enquiries should be made through the publisher.

Cover design: Ultimate World Publishing Cover
Cover photograph: Brad Dennien
Editor: Srah Yuen, Beverly Boorer
Typeset and layout: Ultimate World Publishing

Ultimate World Publishing
Diamond Creek,
Victoria Australia 3089
www.writeabook.com.au

Note from the Author

Expressions of innocence or guilt are my opinion. These expressions are backed by actual life events and/or court rulings. I have deliberately obscured some identifying features of characters in this book for both legal and moral reasons and in some instances dates, locations and other identifiers have been changed to protect those that need protecting. All names have been changed.

In telling my story I am cognisant that I write only my story. I do not presume to tell the story of others who feature predominantly in this book. Their feelings, emotions, thoughts and memories are their own and they deserve the respect I give them by only writing about them what is necessary in telling my own story. This is my perspective only.

This book may trigger painful memories and or unusual reactions, please seek help from someone if this occurs. Please see the back of this book for contact details and help available.

Dedicated to my daughter. My beautiful, strong, engaging, articulate daughter, who takes a central role in my story. You are my child, my daughter, my friend and greatest teacher. What a blessing you are today and every day.

Contents

NOTE FROM THE AUTHOR 3

DEDICATION 5

PROLOGUE 9

CHAPTER ONE—DISILLUSIONED UPBRINGING 13

CHAPTER TWO—TEENAGE TRAUMA AND TENDERNESS 35

CHAPTER THREE—TUMULTUOUS TWENTIES 47

CHAPTER FOUR—THREATENING THIRTIES 95

CHAPTER FIVE—PREDATORY MAN 103

CHAPTER SIX—DAY OF DISCLOSURE 137

CHAPTER SEVEN—THE AFTERMATH 147

CHAPTER EIGHT—THE BEGINNING OF BETTER 181

CHAPTER NINE—THE LONG WAY BACK 217

CHAPTER TEN—LIFE RESILIENCE 227

EPILOGUE 251

ABOUT THE AUTHOR 259

ACKNOWLEDGEMENTS 263

HOTLINES TO HELP 265

REFERENCES 267

Prologue

"If I ever tell you about my past, it's never because I want you to feel sorry for me, but so that you can understand why I am who I am." UNKNOWN

For years I sensed that something was wrong in my life, something was out of alignment, something wasn't quite right. This did not fit the picture of what the world saw and gave commentary to. People I knew coveted my perfect life, commenting on my good fortune of finding a man with so many endearing traits, people were envious of our lives. To all I seemed to have a charmed existence. The bad relationships from the past were over, replaced by a man who loved and adored me and my children, who worked hard in a good job to provide for all of us, a man who raised money for charities, who encouraged me to pursue a career, even if that took me away from my children. A man who could cook and clean and iron and had skills I valued as a working mum. A man who kissed me goodbye each morning, who hugged me and told me he loved me each day. A man who was charming and a good conversationalist.

What an illusion it all was. How I should have listened to those small voices in the back of my head, whispering "it's all too good to be true", "something doesn't add up". The whispers in the chatter of your mind that are designed to destroy the good things in your life. I should have heeded them, but they kept being swept away by my desperation for a happy life and to be loved.

The only indication as to what was about to unfold, was a teenager who went from an innocent pre-teen to a destructive adolescent, prone to violet rants and outbursts. Gone were the innocent conversations of her pre-teen life, to be replaced by verbally abusive rants and outbursts. I expected this from a teenager, to some extent, thought that the developing adolescent in her was testing the world around her, trying to make sense of what her life had been up until that time. The velocity of the outbursts and the depth of her anger worried me though; surely this was not normal.

I attempted to get help from doctors, psychologists and through counsellors. I read and researched everything I could about teenagers, I talked to friends endlessly about the behaviours she was exhibiting and her treatment of me. Her hatred, her disgust of me and her belittling remarks chipped away at my confidence as a mother. I blamed myself for not being able to maintain a balanced relationship with my daughter. I thought that I was a bad mother. It never occurred to me that the issue was not the relationship between us, but the evil that had entered our lives undetected some years earlier, like a cobra; an evil that was envenomating my precious only daughter, doing unspeakable harm. This cobra managed to manipulate me to a point where I thought I was going crazy. Hinting that perhaps I was misinterpreting my daughter's behaviour, that she was normal and I was over reacting; all the while still professing undying love and commitment to me. The confusion of his words took the focus from my daughter and placed it squarely at my feet and had me questioning my right to be a mother at all.

My life up to that point had been a long series of setbacks, of failed relationships, of flawed decision making, hardship and pain. In many ways I had dealt with life as best I could, always searching out ways to succeed instead of fail, trying to right the wrongs and striving to make good from bad. Up to that point I was still dealing with the cards I'd been dealt, and I was a people pleaser.

I wish I'd known such a trait would create a vulnerability that would enable a perpetrator to slip quietly into my life, but worse still, my daughter's life. Now I understand how these evil masters of lies and deception work and I want others to understand too and to be compelled to ask questions.

So much of what happened to me in my life, has been inexplicable. I have suffered hurt, shame, anxiety, depression and fear and felt anger. So much anger. Now that I am older and wiser, I can see why things happened, how things happened. I have an insight into, not only my behaviour, but the behaviour of others. This knowledge has brought me much solace. During each of those turbulent times, it was hard to see past my own emotions and it was only in more settled times that I gained this understanding.

I am not a psychologist, however I have extensively studied psychology and researched endlessly the multitude of science-based articles and books available, to familiarise myself with whatever I was feeling or going through at the time. Together with extensive therapy and counselling, it has combined in such a way as to give me understanding of my reactions, my decision making, my own thoughts and patterns and helped me to heal myself. I'm hoping that it will help to heal others who read this story.

Chapter

Disillusioned upbringing

"It is critical to maintain boundaries between adult problems and children. Please protect your children's innocence and allow them to remain children. They must not be burdened by adult problems. Kids don't have the coping skills or the intellectual ability to understand money worries, adult relationship issues or their parents' unhappiness." JOANNA OESTMANN.

I've thought long and hard about my childhood and found it challenging to put down in words the depths of the feelings I had as a child, into my teenage years and beyond. I've struggled writing about my parents as they were back then, damaged from their own upbringings, bringing up a new generation of children. It is an important part of who I am, so I include it as part of my story, not to apportion blame but to weave it into my account, with all the love and forgiveness I can.

My childhood was plagued by a deep feeling of longing. I longed for happiness, longed to feel safe and secure, longed to feel normal and longed to feel the love of my father. I also felt an overwhelming fear and anxiety, an anxiety so consuming that at times it caused me to physically shake and feel ill to the pit of my stomach. I can honestly say that it was not a happy childhood, though there were moments of happiness in it.

My rural Australian upbringing was typical at that time, or so I thought. Corporal punishment still existed in our schools and we were brought up by a generation that saw harsh punishment as the only way to discipline children.

I would discover later in life, there was so much more that was unusual about our family, rather than usual.

I was the eldest of four children brought up predominately, in the small rural community of Kilkenny in the South Burnett region of South East Queensland, Australia.

I was a stubborn child but open to reasonable requests, provided the request was logical and set out in a way that my inquisitive little brain could articulate. I did not like being told what to do, just because whoever "said so". I needed to understand the why and then compliance with a request was easy. Often there was no explanation and my disobedience resulted in a smack or multiple smacks. Sometimes I was sent to my room to ponder why I was such a "wilful" child.

My endless curiosity for almost any subject ensured that my mind was actively engaged all the time, even as a child. This inherent curiosity caused to me to question my parents often and this was not always met with a caring and intellectual response. If it was my mother I was questioning, all her explanations were based on her deeply held Christian beliefs and usually resulted in the quoting of a biblical verse to back up her reasoning. If it was Dad, then it was met with some silly phrase like "it's a wigwam for a goose's bridle". In other words, he did not know the answer, was too busy to answer or could not be bothered answering correctly.

I have lovely memories of our first home in Romore, Kilkenny. There was a big black wood burning stove in the kitchen that warmed up the whole house. I remember sitting snuggled up under a blanket with slippers, dressing gown and socks, sipping a drink of warm milk. There were cousins who visited and played on my tricycle. A swing that was made from tree logs and chain, ducks in the duck pen and mud puddles to play in. A wonderful big white cat called Snowy who delighted in sleeping in the sun, being snuggled up to me or being carried around by me. He was almost as big as me, but I was tiny as a child.

My earliest memories of my mother centred around her being sick, pregnant or in tears. My mother suffered many miscarriages. There were two miscarriages between my brother and I, one after the birth of my brother and one before the birth of my youngest brother. The loss of one of those babies, whom my mother called Michael, seven months into the pregnancy, upset her the most. In those days a stillborn baby had to be delivered in the maternity ward alongside other expectant mothers giving birth to live babies. The dead baby was then taken from her and there was no record of his birth, no photos, no footprints, no handprints, nothing to acknowledge his arrival but the memory of his birth.

There was nothing to sustain my mother or my father through the grieving process. My heart still breaks for the pain this would have caused them. It must have been very difficult for them to deal with because I was sent away to live with one of my aunties and my brother was sent to be cared for by another relative, for a couple of months. My auntie, Mum's younger sister lived in Brisbane, about two and a half hours away from our family home. Spending time with my aunt, uncle and their three small children was a beautiful memory from my childhood. I felt loved in her home, she listened to me and included me in all that the family did, wrapped me in hugs, warmth and understanding. I have a special place in my heart for her due to the love she showered on me in my childhood.

My mother's desperate pleas for my father's love and attention punctuated the fabric of our lives, as did their arguments. She was needy and desperately insecure at that time in her life and I felt it as a child. It made me feel unsafe and scared a lot of the time. There was a fear that permeated my childhood. At the time it was fear of the dark, fear of the "boogie man", fear of getting in trouble, fear of the switchy stick, fear of doing the wrong thing, fear of my mother's tears, fear of my father's anger. Children need a safe and secure environment to develop and grow. That's not the environment we lived in.

Mum did not have to work outside the home and focussed on being a housewife and running her many charitable organisations and associations for helping others. She also assisted with whatever business enterprise my father was currently delving into. Much of my life up until I left home at seventeen consisted of school, looking after my younger brothers and little sister and the work of running a rural property – mustering, dipping, raising chickens, ducks and geese and the occasional holiday at the beach.

I was an emotional child, a deep thinker and a child who was always comfortable in my own company and being by myself.

I remember often going off by myself to explore the creeks where we lived. I caught yabbies and fish in nets and brought them home to put in the fish tank with the penny turtles I had caught earlier. I was a bit of a tomboy throughout my childhood. I loved to be outside exploring the world and learning about nature and all its infinite beauty. It satisfied the intense curiosity I felt for the world.

My childhood home was filled with a multitude of foster children, recovering relatives and other rescued individuals whom my mother sought to repair. We fostered an abused baby girl, an abused brother and sister, a family of four aboriginal children, a young abused boy, as well as uncles recovering from head injuries, uncles recovering from alcoholism, cousins that were sick as babies, and multitudes of other individuals from around the district. My mother was loved by all and seen as a beacon of light in the community. I often wished it was just us and that we did not have to "share" our mother with so many others.

My childhood was interspersed with severe and harsh punishment, the harshness of which would psychologically scar my siblings and I for life, a dark family "secret" that no one dared to discuss, much less address, at the time it was happening. Bringing it out into the open will no doubt cause pain for those involved but my story cannot be told without it because it impacted me so profoundly; not the actual punishment but the psychological patterning it set in my mind that shaped or rather marred my thinking for years to come.

My brothers and I learnt to "fear" the switchy stick, the leather strap or the poly pipe because of the pain it brought both mentally and physically. I didn't think the severity of these punishments was fair, didn't understand that they were not considered normal.

Most times, the punishments went something like this…..WHACK "do" WHACK "as" WHACK "you" WHACK "are" WHACK "told" WHACK, "or" WHACK "you" WHACK "will" WHACK "be" WHACK "smacked" WHACK "till" WHACK "you" WHACK" cant" WHACK "sit" WHACK "down".

I lost count of how many times during primary school I would go to school with big red welts across the tops of my legs and my bottom. I would spend the day desperately trying to make sure that no one noticed the ones on my legs and no one saw my shame. I'd pull my uniform down or try to wear long pants, even if it was the middle of summer. It was torture just sitting down. I'm not sure what the punishments were for, maybe answering back, maybe not doing as I was told, I can't really remember, but I remember the thick welts of bruises and just how long they seemed to last.

The physical pain would fade long before the deep-seated anger and at times, hatred, I felt towards my father or my mother. A fact that made me so ashamed, as I thought everyone loved their parents and how lucky was I to have parents at all.

One of the most humiliating aspects of our punishment was having to pull down our pants or having them forcibly pulled down so that the implement of our punishment, be that a strap or a wooden spoon or whatever implement was handy at the time, could strike the skin of our bare bottoms or legs. That stinging, burning pain that caused you to yell and scream and then resulted in more smacks for screaming. After our punishment was finished, my mother would expect us to hug our father or if she was the dispenser of the punishment, we had to hug her, like somehow our hugging absolved the parent from the "hiding" we'd had. We had to take our punishment and get over it. I don't think any of us got over it.

The injustice of these beatings would cause me to try and run away from home before I was even ten. I packed up a little bag with pyjamas and clothes and lowered it outside my bedroom window. Then I realised that I could not drop out the window, as I was too short and hastily made my way out the back door to collect my bag. My mother caught me a few hundred metres from home, after a neighbour alerted her to my escape. She just laughed at me and something in my soul started to die then. I felt like no one cared and no one would listen, no one would save me.

In my conflicted upbringing, I never witnessed physical abuse between my parents, but the verbal arguments were not what young impressionable ears should bear witness to. Our home was like a battlefield where conflict arose at every corner of our lives. Most of the conflict arose from my mother's insistence that we follow a true and proper Christian upbringing and my father's distaste of religion and Christianity in general. My father's taunts of "don't be so bloody stupid", to my mother, make me cringe today, but back then they just made me cower in fear. My mother clung to her faith as if it was saving her life. All I ever saw it do was create deep division in our lives. She steadfastly clung to the hope that my father would change his views, but he never has, and I doubt he ever will.

I bonded closely with my immediate younger brother, bore the brunt of responsibility for my mischief making littlest brother and adored my baby sister.

My adopted baby sister was and is the delight of my life. I took on a mothering role more than that of a big sister. I was that much older and was able to participate in looking after her until I left home. By the time my parents got to her, her upbringing was completely different, and she benefited from a completely different relationship with my father by that stage. He had mellowed and managed to have a better father-daughter relationship with her. My youngest and only sister benefited from my parent's extensive experience in raising their own children and other foster children, by the time they adopted her. They were older, wiser and gentler on her than they were on us. We all spoilt her and treated her as the gift she was in our lives.

My mother and I shared, what I thought was a close relationship, however this was very much one-sided. Because she did not get what she needed from my father, in terms of emotional support, she clung to me and used me as a listening post and sounding board for information and concepts I couldn't understand. When I was in primary school, she talked to me about her fear that my father was having an affair with a woman who lived in the caretaker's house on our property. I remember the confusion I felt and the fear her tears caused in my heart. I also knew about affairs of our other relatives without even knowing what an affair was, just knowing it was wrong. I think even then, I knew boundaries had been breached.

I felt I had no room to grow and learn on my own, my thoughts were her thoughts, my actions her actions, my beliefs her beliefs. Even if I started to question any of it, her tears and tantrums caused me to give up having any ideas contrary to her own. The pain of seeing her in tears always stopped any independent thought I had.

I, on the other hand, had a desperate need to be loved by her and to do everything she wanted, even if that was to my own detriment. I have wondered, among other things, why she did not protect us from the harsh punishments we received.

I knew from an early age that my mother had been molested. She told me in primary school at about the time we started to have an awareness of "stranger danger". I did not find out until I was much older that her molester was her father. My mother's father, by all accounts, came home from the second world war a changed and damaged man. His alleged offenses against his daughters were kept from their own mother and the world until much later in their lives.

Mum's younger brother also abused my mother's sisters. There was and is so much secrecy surrounding what happened in the family. The secrecy on my mother's side of the family stifled the truth from ever coming out and in doing so protected the perpetrators of sin.

When I discovered more details of what had happened to my mother and aunts, I wondered why my mother had remained in contact with the male members of her family and allowed them to be anywhere near her own children. I wondered why she did not have the courage to make the break from them, to cut them out of her life completely.

My mother was the 3rd eldest of 11 children. I know too that grandfather was a bit of a tyrant who made all the children work extraordinarily hard on the small crop farm where they grew up. They had very little money and too many mouths to feed, which resulted in the oldest children leaving home at 14, 15 and 16 years of age to support the rest of the family.

My father was the product of a long lineage of Smiths, who arrived in Australia as convicts from the British Empire. The second eldest in a family of three and the only boy, his story is one of family tradition and family expectation. The family property, "Live and Let Live" at Kilkenny, in the South Burnett region of Queensland, had been in the family for three generations by the time Dad had enough money to purchase it for himself and I'm not sure that it was what he really wanted for his life. The story around the family property is also surrounded in secrecy, much of which I am not privy to. You see, Grandad Smith insisted that the girls, my father's two sisters, received the exact same dollar value in money and assets as Dad did, but somehow Dad had to pay for his share. It was almost like he inherited the right to buy the family property, with the compounding expectation that he would do so, even if he didn't want to. The property was a substantial parcel of land that had been used for all sorts of farming enterprises from dairying to cropping to beef cattle and grazing. It was also rich with alluvial gold deposits. Unfortunately, as a landowner, you don't own what's under the ground only what's above it. So that was never any help out of our dire family financial situation.

Instead of the property bringing with it a rich tapestry of family history, it seemed more to be a noose around his neck. It was one of the causes of endless arguments between my mother and father. The land was prone to drought conditions and always dry. The creeks only ran seasonally, and my parents always struggled to make ends meet. Dad often had to take work outside the farm to earn money to keep us all fed and clothed. When other farming families had motorbikes and farm utes, we had horses and walked.

My father did not seem to enjoy the farming life, he was always angry, or so it seemed, when I was growing up. I now know that my father suffered and still suffers from depression and anxiety. Never diagnosed, but I know the symptoms intimately and I see them in his life back then, as I do now. I know from the way he has helped me with my own battles with depression and anxiety, the understanding he shows can only be shown by someone who knows what it is like to struggle with these diagnoses.

I never felt close to my father whilst I was growing up. In fact, I was 21 years old before my father even told me he loved me. I was surprised and shocked to hear him say it out loud. We never had a close physical relationship, no hugs, no father-daughter closeness. Unless Mum intervened and insisted that I hug him or sit on his knee, show some level of physical closeness. Those moments caused me so much uneasiness, I loathed them and longed for a way out of the awkwardness of it all. Listening to the many conversations about inappropriate touching and what had happened to my mother, somehow contributed to the fear I felt from most other men in and around me, as a child. Perhaps he was too young to be a dad and just never knew how to react, indeed my mother hinted that Grandad Smith was a better grandfather than he had ever been a father.

The most loving and unconditionally supportive people in my life, were my grandad and Nana Smith, my father's parents. I knew I was grandad's favourite and I knew that from him I could receive unlimited cuddles and hugs, love and understanding. This is as it should be with all grandparents. If there was ever a place to escape to it was Grandad and Nannas' and even from a young age I would do just that. Once when I was about seven, I fell sick at school, or perhaps I just wanted some attention from Nana. I knew that my mother was in

Gymthorpe, (the closest major city to us, some 45 minutes away from Kilkenny), all day and would not be home until later that afternoon. When the school tried to contact her to come and pick me up, they could not get in contact with her, so I suggested that as Nanna just lived across the road from the school, perhaps I could go to Nana's and have a lie down. All very innocent and thoughtful for a child of seven but when Mum arrived to pick me up, the resultant argument she had with Nana was neither pleasant nor just. Apparently, I should have stayed at school and waited for my mother to return.

My mother never liked the close association we had with the Smith grandparents. She was critical of my Granddad and appeared jealous of my Nanna. Her own insecurity seemed to see any relationship between my father and his mother as a slight on her own relationship with my father. He fought with Mum endlessly about his parents. This in turn caused us to cling to Mum, because we had no one else. She did not protect us from his wrath, but we still clung to her in the mistaken hope that she would intervene at some stage. Conversations later in life revealed that there were indeed times when she felt she should have intervened but never did. Her absolute faith in God and the biblical verses that place the husband as the head of the household seemed to keep her stuck in this environment, defensive of her husband and loyal to him at all costs.

I felt safe wrapped in Grandad's strong arms on his knee, but even this space was tainted by my mother's "stranger danger" and "inappropriate touching" talks. What should have been a safe and pure place of escape for me was forever tinged with uncertainty from a little mind that couldn't quite understand. I know that children must be kept safe and that's what my mother was trying to do, but it was the other grandfather that we needed to be kept safe from and not Granddad Smith. He often questioned our punishments, which made me love him even more, but made my parents even angrier. The last words he ever spoke were to tell me he loved me and just how proud he was of me. He was a big strong man and wonderful influence in my life, my protector, my friend, my Grandad. I loved my Grandad with all my heart and I miss him to this day, some 25 plus years after his death.

My deep-seated insecurities and low self-esteem also arose from an early childhood spent in and out of hospital.

I was born with a lower left preauricular sinus which travelled from my parotoid gland to the left lower ear. Put simply I had a tiny hole, just inside my ear, near my earlobe, which was connected all the way to my salivary glands. It's classified as a congenital birth defect. Mine was prone to infections and required multiple surgeries to repair.

After one surgery, the subsequent infection damaged my left side facial nerve, leaving me with permanent facial palsy. This vital little nerve is responsible for so many facial functions including smiling, raising your eyebrows, wriggling your nose, winking and whistling. Most people take these expressions for granted but I have always struggled with them or am completely unable to perform them. To this day, I cannot raise my eyebrow on the left-hand side, cannot wink with my left eye and can't whistle properly. The ability to smile is one of life's great gifts. The very act of smiling makes you feel better, and certainly makes you look more attractive. Not being able to smile properly had a huge impact on my life.

It makes simple tasks like cleaning your teeth difficult and to this day I use my hand to seal my mouth when rinsing my teeth. It is also responsible for maintaining a healthy eye with a continual flow of tears. Aside from drying out, prolonged loss of tears can cause the formation of ulcers on the cornea. Using artificial tears and the insertion of a small tube in my tear duct helps with these issues. The effects of gravity cause the face on that side to "droop". Permanent facial palsy caused both physical and mental pain throughout childhood and into adult life.

There were also endless trips to the dentist.

I had a small jaw and too many teeth, which required removal. When all my baby teeth fell out, they would be replaced by tetracycline stained and damaged permanent teeth. Tetracycline staining of the teeth left them yellow/grey with a visible indent where the new white enamel of the teeth should have been. It was the antibiotic of choice to fight the serious nature of the infections I had as a baby and toddler. The tetracycline binds to the non-erupted teeth and once the teeth come through, they are yellowed in colour. Then when the light hits the teeth it causes the tetracycline to oxidise and turns the teeth a grey/yellow. It's now banned for use, except in extreme circumstances, in all small children.

Yet another reason not to look in the mirror and smile or enjoy photographs being taken.

Interestingly there has been a lifelong regeneration of the nerves around my lower mouth, however my left eye remains prone to "laziness" and is most noticeable when I'm tired. The comparison between my face as a young child and my face as a middle-aged woman is quite remarkable. I now have an almost normal smile, complete with a left sided dimple on my lower cheek. The right side of my face tends to pull the smile more to the right, but if I'm conscious of my smile I can manage it so that the right side pulls less and equals the left side. The improvement has been life changing for me and I love to laugh and smile now, despite what has happened in my life.

I was subjected to intense bullying throughout my childhood and suffered a powerful lack of self-esteem which plagued me throughout my life.

I remember the first day of school. My little blue school port (school bag) with brown plastic corner protectors, packed with a jam sandwich wrapped in wax paper, an apple, a couple of books and my new crayons and pencils, ready to start school. I was so excited to be going to school, happy to be meeting new kids and starting to learn.

I adored my teacher, Miss Bycroft. She was so tall and slim, a beautiful woman and kind as well. I remember the exact moment my delight at being in school turned to tears. Leonardo, the boy who shouted loudly across the room "what's wrong with your face?". My childhood tormentor!

I vaguely remember that Miss Bycroft said kind words to me and instructed the other kids not to make fun of me, that I could not smile like other children, that this wasn't my fault. I discovered years later that Leonardo's childhood was pretty messed up, so I forgave him for his harsh words, his jibes, tormenting ways and physical pushes and punches. But it still stung back then.

Being a small community, some of the teachers at Kilkenny Primary School were often the mothers of children at the school or related to the children in some way. I learnt firsthand that this was not the best thing for me. One of my teachers in middle primary school took a dislike to me and it turned out she was my Dad's cousin. I'm not sure if my father had caused his cousin harm in some way during their childhood but whatever it was, she certainly gave me a hard time. I've always felt there were bigger darker family issues that caused her to be as mean to me as she was.

Her bullying is the strongest and most enduring of my memories from primary school. The bullying, the punishment and the way she spoke to me would leave lasting mental anguish. I spent my primary years trying to stay out of her way, but she taught me for three of those years and went out of her way to belittle me during the other years of primary school. I look back at some of the things I suffered because of her and cringe. I remember crying myself to sleep because of her, begging my parents to help, which they tried to elicit on my behalf, on a few occasions. This only made her worse and I stopped telling my parents in the mistaken belief that perhaps I was better off dealing with her myself.

A couple of the most traumatic bullying instances occurred when I was ten and twelve years of age and no longer in any of her classes. I was a tomboy and even then, I got on better with boys than I did with girls. I had started enjoying the lunch time cricket games with the boys and loved it. The boys chose me on one of their teams and I felt like an equal; what I looked like didn't matter, catching the cricket ball did. During one lunchtime game I was hauled off the ground by my nemesis and dragged back up to the classroom. She yelled at me for playing cricket with the boys, belittling me to the point where I was crying, in those huge, all of body, air gulping sobs that only 10-year olds, have the capacity for. The principal walked in at about this time and that stopped her in her tracks. I was so relieved that someone had arrived to save me from her savagery. But then she lied to him. I was incredulous!

Even as an adult writing this I'm appalled by her behaviour. She said that I was in trouble for littering and that I was being punished. The kindly principal looked to me and asked if this was true. I pleaded my innocence and started to explain about the cricket, when she intervened and said she was dealing with it and with that the principal left the two of us alone. I was banned from playing cricket. I was devastated. It was also the first time I discovered that adults lie. What upset me more was that one of her favourites, a beautiful girl with red hair, took my place. I must admit to the horrid teasing I inflicted on this beautiful girl; it was wrong, and I am sorry but 10 year olds don't have the capacity to understand the pain their teasing inflicts unless they have an in-tune adult to explain this to them and I didn't. I only gave out what was directed at me and I knew no other way than to give back the teasing that I received endlessly.

Not only was this woman a teacher at the school, but she also ran the school band, which I was part of. I liked being in the school band. It was an opportunity to travel across the country performing and it was a great social time for a primary aged child. It was only ever marred by her snide comments and derogatory rebukes of me.

There were many other instances of her bullying and yelling at me but there was a second incident that particularly sticks in my memory. In Grade 7, we girls had the opportunity to make our debut. The debutante ball was the highlight of the end of primary school. We got to pick our partners, get special dresses and go to dancing lessons. It was exciting and it was fun. I had a crush on the "most handsome boy in the school", Rodney. His family and my family knew each other and even though it was before the years where "going steady" was considered a "thing", he was my first boy crush. We passed each other notes in school and hung out during breaks. I'd watch him play cricket from the sidelines. All so delightfully innocent. We never even held hands or kissed. Anyway, he was my partner for the debutante ball.

We practiced our dances at lessons for weeks before the ball, but unfortunately my nemesis teacher, was in charge of the dancing lessons. About a week before the ball, she decided that I would no longer partner Rodney in the school ball, but that Helena, the "beautiful red-haired girl" would. She was taller, prettier than I was and so should be partnered with Rodney. I can't even remember who she placed me with, only that is wasn't him. Again, I was so devastated and as I started to cry and protest, I was told to get on with the lesson or go sit outside and wait for my parents. This time I told my parents what had happened and this time they intervened on my behalf. Rodney's parents agreed and after phone calls between the two parents we were partnered together again. Not without a few snide comments on the night from her. Why would you say to a 12yr old that "it's a shame you insisted on partnering Rodney, he was much better suited to Helena".

I have heard many others that went to the same school, speak so lovingly of her. Indeed, she was dearly loved by her family. This was not my experience with her, but it does demonstrate that people are multi-dimensional, and that one person can dislike and bully you and love another quite easily.

Growing up on a larger property I had to work hard and take on responsibility beyond my years. As the eldest it often fell to me to look after my younger brothers and sister and attend to the many household chores. Before I was twelve I could cook, clean, wash, iron and look after the household. It was also my role to help with all the foster children as well. There were times where there would be up to eight children in the household under the age of twelve, four of us and four of them. I really wondered why my parents were allowed to have foster children, they got the same floggings as we did, in some instances.

Another remnant of our childhood was my association with food. We had to eat everything on our plates, no matter what it was. Anyone who's ever been forced to eat tripe as an unwilling child, will know what I mean. To try and forcibly eat something that makes you retch uncontrollably is a horrific experience and one I have not repeated with my own children. I'm sure it stems from the Great Depression and times of food shortage, but it's not necessary now and wasn't necessary then, not in modern times. Children will eat when they are hungry and should never be forced to eat something that makes them physically sick. The psychological impact is one that causes over-eating and an unconscious need to finish everything on your plate, even when you are full.

Chapter Two

Teenage trauma and tenderness

"The first time you fall in love it changes you forever and no matter how hard you try, that feeling never goes away". NICHOLAS SPARKS

I remember very clearly the first time I tried, rather pitifully, to take my own life. I had been studying for an upcoming exam and my parents were taking my brothers to athletics training in the nearby township of Gymthorpe, about a 45-minute drive in those days. I wanted to stay home and have some down time, finish my study. I wasn't allowed to. To this day I can still feel the anger and rage boil up inside me, when I think of that moment. It seems so futile now, so petty, but I just wanted some time out and they insisted I come with them to the athletics. It meant that I would lose about four hours of study time and school was important to me then. As I went to go to the car, I grabbed a pair of scissors. I tried to cut my wrists with those blunt old scissors. Luckily, they were so blunt, that all I was left with were red marks where I'd tried. Though this is not an isolated incident in a lot of teenager's lives, it was my first real cry for help. A cry no one heard, and no one knew about, until now. I can look back and feel compassion for the teenage me, trying desperately to have some time out from the family battles. I would learn that it was useless to go against my parents' wishes, for they had control and that I had no power to make decisions for myself. It took me a long time to find out that I was able to make good, strong decisions on my own.

Junior high school was not too far removed from primary school, in fact, barely fifty metres separated the two schools. The transition to high school was an easy one for me. I thrived on the variety of subjects we could now do. There were a few new students, but many of those I started school with continued with me into high school. In my grade there was only four girls. This meant that we spent most of the time hanging out together and some of those friendships forged then, still flourish today. High school was reasonably carefree, whilst I was at school. The teasing and bullying of primary school had lessened, but was still present from time to time. Boys become a fascination and whilst many of my friends were having first boyfriends, I just looked on from a distance. The most outrageous thing I ever did was get a photo taken of me with a cigarette in my hand....it was just for show but to this day my Mum still thinks that I had been smoking. A nasty habit I didn't take up until night duty nursing at 19 years of age.

One of our rare holidays at Coolum on the Sunshine Coast, in Queensland was seared into my memory. My brothers and I had been walking along the beach. My little sister was too little to be with us and remained at home with Mum. Unbeknown to me, my brothers had turned to go home, but I continued on alone, totally oblivious to the fact that I was now alone on the beach apart from a few other adults and a couple of kids. Even back then I relished time alone, loved it, craved it. It was not a "naughty" thing. I learnt later in life that I need to rejuvenate myself by quiet time alone, but back then I just knew I needed some time away from the other family members and the angst that being together as a family meant. I don't ever remember feeling comfortable at home, you know, that "Sunday night in your pyjamas comfortable", where home is a great space to be.

That afternoon on the beach at Coolum, all I knew was that my angry father was yelling at me to come home and chasing me down the beach, switchy stick in hand, swiping and hitting me all the way home. (A switchy stick was a long, thin, flexible, piece of branch, plucked from any available tree, with all the small branches and foliage removed. Its flexibility meant that it stung like a wasp when it met the skin.) It would have been about a kilometre along the beach and back up to the house. Upon returning home, my tear streaked face looked to my mother for help. Shaking her head, she said that I should have known to come home as soon as the boys returned home. It was no one's fault but my own that I had been flogged in view of anyone on that stretch of beach, across the road and back up to the beach house where we were staying. I was so angry, so humiliated and so disgusted that I was being treated this way. Why did no one care enough to save me from this pain? My fourteen yrs old self decided then and there to be out of home as soon as I could.

It was during my high school years that Mum and Dad purchased a holiday house at Woodgate. This house became the centre of fun and frivolity over the years for us kids and all the other local children that congregated there on school holidays. We especially had fun when Mum and Dad weren't around. We, my brothers and I, had bikes and kayaks and we could "escape". There was an overwhelming sense of freedom at Woodgate. We left home early, came home for lunch and went off again only to return in time for tea. We had bonfires on the beach, walked for miles and met all the other holiday house owners' kids along the way. Wonderful memories of carefree days at the beach, the smell of the bonfires made from coastal trees, the blueness of the ocean as it stretched out before us to the horizon, fishing off the beach, but most of all we had freedom. The tension we children experienced at home, seemed to evaporate as soon as we got to Woodgate. Our little moments of blue sky in an otherwise cloudy universe.

My need for personal space would cause friction in the home throughout my teenage years as my mother did not understand my need for personal space and had little respect for it or my need for privacy. I remember the day, in my teens, that I discovered she had been reading my diaries, and how angry I was. I did not have anything to hide but felt that she had taken away the last little bit of me that was private. That private, soul searching teenager who had begun to build a life outside of the family home, the me I had carefully woven into the pages of those diaries, where I thought no one would see, where I thought I was safe.

Up until I went to senior high school, life was emotionally turbulent at home. My years at senior high school were wonderful years though, some of the best of my life. Filled with learning, friends, football and love. I had to go to a regional high school requiring an hour-long bus ride each morning. So, at almost 16, I was up at 6am and on the bus by 7.30am each morning after the 15-minute drive to Kilkenny to catch the bus. This big old yellow bus with red seats and steel handrails was driven by a creepy old man, who unfortunately, later turned out to be the paedophile we all thought he looked like. Not that we conceptualized that at the time. It was tiring and the trip home after school was always a fight to stay awake. By the time I got home, did my afternoon chores, had tea and studied for a few hours it was time for bed, only to start all over again. I was essentially out of the house and away from the angst of life at home.

Murgon High School was a wonderful place for a senior education. We had fabulous teachers who were engaged in making our senior years a stepping stone to the world beyond. I loved what there was to learn apart from having to take Maths II. I loathed Maths II, a first for me and I was not good at this subject at all. My father had insisted I take that subject, I'm not sure why.

We had lots of committees which drove all sorts of fun activities for the senior students. There were musicals, sporting events and lots of new people to meet. I was part of the Cultural Committee and it was a blast! We organised bus trips to theme parks, football games and to the Glitter Coast beaches. How on earth we got to do this is beyond me today, but it was so much fun back then. It was here that the infancy of my organisational skills were learnt. It was also a time of cementing friendships and learning about love. I discovered that there was a great reason to stay in the Maths II class. Not only did I like my teacher, who was also the high school football coach, there was also a particularly nice boy in my class. He would become the "first love" of my life.

Andrew was the son of a local farmer and a primary school teacher. The third boy in a family of six boys and one girl. He was tall, handsome and very smart. We started talking in class and soon realised how much we liked each other. Talking in class progressed to talking for hours after school. In those days there were only landlines, so being on the phone for hours at night was cause for some arguments with my parents. We had the foundations of a great friendship; with similar upbringing there was a shared understanding. I experienced the butterflies that only first love can bring. It was such a happy time. I couldn't believe that this handsome, football playing giant of a guy liked "little old me" with the crooked smile and a mouth full of braces. Having a mouth full of braces does make sharing first kisses a little difficult, but as teenagers you manage. He played in the winning State football team and there was so much fun to be had going on the footy trips with the team. With this boy I felt loved, protected, cherished and cared for and because I felt all these things it would eventually cause me to run as far and fast as I could, for fear that I was not good enough and that he might see the real me, the broken, hurt, scared, insecure me.

During high school I started to experience the first of many episodes of ovarian cysts; a condition called polycystic ovaries. The intense pain would come from out of nowhere and have me bend in two, curled up in a ball on my bed rocking myself in pain. It was often accompanied with a fever and vomiting. The intensity of the pain would almost make me pass out and I knew before long what the beginning of an attack felt like. It would start with an intense nausea that was soon replaced by steadily increasing levels of stabbing pain and cold sweats. Many times, I just lay on the bed waiting for it to pass, which usually it did. Mum would give me Panadol and hot packs to ease the pain, but usually they had no effect whatsoever.

The worst episode had me feeling like I was about to die and begging Mum to take me to a doctor. I was about 16 at the time. When I finally reached the hospital, it was a quick trip to the operating theatre with a suspected burst ovarian cyst. I was incredibly ill and exceedingly lucky that I made it to the hospital to have the laparoscopy in time. After that episode it was decided that I needed to take the "pill" to control the hormones which led to the development of the cysts.

The decision to put me on the pill was a disastrous decision in terms of my mental health. I had always been led to believe that only "tramps" took the pill; girls who wanted to have sex outside of marriage. My mother's Christian beliefs were my own at that stage of life. I had not had the opportunity to develop any of my own theories on religion or what my beliefs were. This belief system was now in direct conflict with what she was making me do. It was my first conscious knowledge of hypocrisy, or so my immature mind thought at the time. The reality was that the hormones in the pill would control the formation of the cysts that had the potential to threaten my life and my reproductive future. All I understood was, that somehow, I was now in a class with tramps and promiscuous young girls and my already low self-esteem just plummeted well below normal. This hormonal cocktail also contributed to my developing depression.

Understanding the influence of my mother and father is very important in my story. I had learnt that to go against my mother would result in her manipulating me into doing what she wanted anyway or crying until I did what she required. To go against my father resulted in a horrible verbal argument or a physical beating. In my case, my response to the control of my parents was to identify closely with their beliefs and belief systems. I thought what they did, had the same prejudices they had, did what they thought I should do. Well, on the surface at least, underneath I battled with the voices of reason in my mind.

The consequences of a daughter not having a loving relationship with her father are far reaching. A woman's "early relationship with her dad, who is usually the first male object of her love, shapes her conscious and unconscious perceptions of what she can expect and what is acceptable in a romantic partner." Based on my childhood, my adult relationships would be abusive, lacking in physical touch or demonstrations of love and affection, volatile and unhealthy. Unfortunately, that's pretty much what I chose in my twenties and thirties. There is no blame in this story, just an acknowledgement that there was no chance of changing my future choices without access to therapy and an understanding of the battles I would face. My unconscious thinking had been well formed by this stage and I would go on to prove all the research right. The abuse cycle had been set in my unconscious brain and would play out across my life until I sought the therapy I needed to heal.

My father is not the same person now. The years have mellowed him and time has healed me. I have long forgiven the hurt. Slowly and over the decades since my childhood I have seen my father grow, evolve and change from the man I knew back then. He has walked beside me through many of the traumas of my later life, showed an understanding of what I was going through and a depth of love I didn't know he had. He's my Dad and I love him.

At the end of high school, I was looking at what to do with my life. I was keen to leave home but in no position to do so unless I had a job. I applied for various bank roles whilst awaiting the outcome of my (Tertiary Education) TE score and offers of university placement. I was lost and not sure of what I wanted to do. At that time my mother insisted that I apply for unemployment benefits – I found this humiliating. I was seventeen and had been brought up on a solid rhetoric that insisted all people on unemployment benefits were "bludgers" and now here was my mother insisting that I apply and start bringing in money to support myself. I was mortified, yet another hit to the self-esteem. With proper discussion and understanding this would not have been a problem but again I felt abandoned and humiliated. Not long after this I received a "you haven't" got the job letter, making me even more miserable.

One of the other options at the time was nursing, so I applied for that role as well. All my friends from school were busying themselves getting ready to move to Brisbane and to go to university or college. I felt really left out. Then I received a letter stating I'd been successful with my application to get into nursing and an acceptance to start university studying Psychology. Nursing was due to start in May and university was to start in February. Before I could think too much further on what I was to do, I received another letter asking if I wanted to start nursing in Gymthorpe in that January. I deferred my psychology course and started nursing in January 1986. Retrospectively, the psychology course would have been much more help to me, but the nursing offered the fastest way out of home.

My church upbringing had a lot to answer for in terms of fitting in with the outside world. My entry to nursing at the age of 17 was the first time I'd been away from home and the home sickness I felt was all consuming. I know it sounds strange to miss such a dysfunctional home but for me, dysfunction was my normal and I missed my siblings. I felt so alone and lost, isolated from all I knew and ill-equipped or prepared for a life outside the family home. Yes, I had practical skills but little in terms of the social skills required to move from the isolated rural upbringing I'd had, to the bustling regional centre of Gymthorpe, where my nursing training commenced. This compounded the insecurity I felt and I didn't feel comfortable in the world in which I found myself. I did not know how to gauge my reaction to alcohol, I did not have any understanding of social norms, I didn't know how to dress to fit in, I was so lost. My parents' influence seemed to grow stronger the older I got, and it would be many years before I learnt to tackle life as my own person, in my own way.

It was the beginning of twenty years hard labour in the world.

TONI LONTIS

Chapter Three

Tumultuous twenties

"In your twenties, if you have any amount of complexity in your childhood, or any trauma that you haven't dealt with, it comes out. That's why you have a lot of artists that don't make it through".
JEREMY SISTO

In her book, Trauma and Recovery, Judith Lewis Herman, talks about "the personality formed in the environment of coercive control is not well adapted to adult life. The survivor is left with fundamental problems in basic trust, autonomy, and intuition. She approaches every task of early adulthood, establishing independence and intimacy, burdened by major impairments in self-care, in cognition, and in memory, in identity and in the capacity to form stable relationships. She is still a prisoner of her childhood; attempting to create a new life, she re-encounters trauma."

My adult retrospective therapy and research have given me an understanding of my behaviour; the "why" if you like, that I was attracted to men not deserving of me; why I tolerated such bad behaviour from the men in and around my life and why I made such bad decisions. Some of these learnings are, of course, part of normal growing up and life discovery but most were due to my desperate need for love and acceptance, my dysfunctional family relationships and my own insecurities.Living in the microcosm of a rural country town where nobody minds their own business made everything harder and put a spotlight on my shortcomings. I would have been much better off moving to Brisbane with my classmates and learning and making mistakes amongst the friends I knew, loved and trusted.

During that time, hospital-based nursing training was the norm in Australia. By the time I finished three years later, it was being phased out and replaced by the university training that remains today. Hospital-based training required young nurses to live in the nursing quarters onsite for at least the first twelve months. These general hospitals, with nurse quarters and nurses training facilities, were part of the fabric of most rural and regional communities at the time. The training consisted of blocks of lectures, assignments and/or exams coupled with blocks of full-time work in the wards and specialty areas such as the emergency department, operating theatres, maternity, and paediatrics. Gymthorpe was renowned at that time for the depth and variety of training opportunities it provided to its nurses and many graduating Gymthorpe nurses went on to have prestigious nursing careers across the country.

It should have been an exciting and fulfilling time for me. However much of what happened during those training years only served to increase the existing insecurities I already felt. It was a time in nursing where the Matron still had 'sway' over what trainee nurses did in terms of time off, pass outs from the nurse's quarters and the night curfew. The whole three years could be seen as very draconian by today's standards. Trainee nurses were also subjected to some terrible bullying by older nurses and heads of departments, including medical staff. Doctors were not questioned even if you knew they were wrong; what they said always stood. Healthcare back then was not the collaborative approach we enjoy today.

During these training years, some of the mistakes I made set in place a sequence of events, due to learned behaviour, which would take me years and years to reset. It would also create the vulnerability in me which enabled a predator to hone in on my child.

One of the first of these mistakes was to break up with Andrew, my long-term, high school sweetheart. My mother still had so much influence over me. Instead of them letting me learn about boyfriends and partners for myself, she interfered where Andrew was concerned.

Had I had the maturity to stick with Andrew, I may have been able to break the cycle of abuse in my life much earlier, with therapy and a loving and supportive relationship. However, my perceptions and tolerances were made up of unconscious thought patterns and conditioning. So even if I thought Andrew was good for me in terms of a long-term relationship, I neither had the skills nor unconscious reasoning to successfully negotiate a positive relationship with him. My feelings of low self-esteem and feeling deeply unworthy destroyed this for me.

My mother believed that someone else was "the one", like some antiquated romance novel, convinced there was only one person in all the universe that could be a partner for life. I wish I had relied on my own intuition rather than my mother's view of the world. I was also lonely because Andrew was in Brisbane with all my high school friends and I was stuck in Gymthorpe. This was a time before the internet, email and mobile phones, so letters were the main method of communication, taking days to arrive. Had I had my friends and Andrew around me, it would no doubt have insulated me against the stresses of life as a naïve young adult and been a buffer against my mother's influence. But I felt abandoned, ill-prepared and desperately homesick, missing my friends and missing my boyfriend.

Andrew was deeply distressed that I decided to call off the relationship.

"He would have done anything", he said, "for us to stay together". I just did not see how we could when I believed my mother knew best.

I could not know the toll that the decision to end this relationship would have on me, nor its long-term consequences.

The strong, safe, supported stability and unconditional love offered by Andrew, was now replaced by nothing but a hope that someone my mother thought was perfect for me, would become part of my life in some real way.

Daniel and I met in our early teens through the church youth group, when I was about 14 years old. My mother had encouraged our friendship from the beginning, as she had dated one of Daniel's uncles in her teenage years.

Daniel was the son of a fellow church parishioner at my mother's church. His mother was a single parent of five children. His Dad had died from lung cancer. They had relied on their belief in God and expected him to be healed by God, but they were let down by their beliefs. Daniel was only 15 years old when his father passed and the thriving family business, running milk tanker trucks had to be sold to support the family.

I had gone through everything that had happened to Daniel's family because they were part of the church that we went to. I was also friends with his younger sister, Beth.

Daniel and I had a brief teenage romance which survived on a few letters and the occasional phone call to each other. We never actually went on any dates during that time. We didn't live in the same town and only saw each other at church, at the youth group, youth camp or the occasional family visit. Daniel decided to move out to Western Queensland to pursue work at the age of 16 so our pseudo-romance came to an end. As the oldest boy in the family, it fell to him to help support his mother financially. I was devastated at the time and I had a distant hope that he would one day return and we could pick up where we left off.

I went on to meet and fall in love with Andrew in senior high school and learned what real romance should look like, and how I should feel when I cared for someone deeply.

With Andrew and I now apart, the opportunity came for Daniel and I to reunite. Daniel was home for holidays and came to pay a visit to the family farm in Kilkenny. It was lovely to see him, but it was not earth-shattering. The second time around would prove to be no different from our first-round romance. I could not seem to get two words out of him, which wasn't promising.

I can't remember if we ever even went on a date. It was just accepted and expected by the church and our families, that Daniel and I were together now and therefore a couple. I was never really sure where I stood in this relationship. I'd had more dates, more quality time with Andrew than I ever did with Daniel, but I felt obligated to Daniel, thought that with enough love and understanding he could and would change.

Daniel still lived thousands of kilometres away, in the mining town of Thargomindah, in outback Queensland, but whereas Andrew easily communicated with me during our time apart, Daniel failed to communicate even when he was standing two feet away.

Daniel was battling his own private demons. He also didn't seem to need to make an effort for me; perhaps he did not know how? He just expected that I would be there, at home waiting for him, when he returned twelve months later for his annual holiday.

It was pretty much pre-ordained that Daniel and I would marry, passion or no passion. My mother decreed it. My brothers were particularly fond of Daniel too, but looking back that was hardly a reason to have a relationship with someone.

Something happened prior to Daniel's return home.

Ben went to the youth group at the church that I still attended in my spare time. I was immediately out of my depth with him, having only ever experienced the safety of uncomplicated young love. I was attracted to him, but more importantly, he was there and not halfway across the country.

I trusted Ben because he went to church. So I placed myself in a position which enabled Ben to take from me something that was precious, without so much as asking; something that can only be taken once, something that should only be taken in circumstances of mutual agreement and trust and a loving relationship. This is not what Ben and I had.

What should have been a lovely memory to carry through life was a bad memory. I had not wanted to lose my virginity that night, but my feeble attempts at saying no seemed futile. Ben did not respect my wishes, told me that it was all right to be nervous and ultimately, I just gave in. That moment became a catalyst for decades of self-loathing because I had allowed myself to be taken outside of marriage. It had little to do with the actual event, but more to do with my religious upbringing that skewed reality and had me believing that sex before marriage was utterly wrong and that now I was dirty, not worthy of the love I so desperately sought. These beliefs have little to do with the reality of a desirable young woman becoming an adult in a regional community where chances were that it would happen with or without my consent.

What made it worse was my mother's discovery of the fact that I was no longer a "wholesome" young girl. The church rumour mill had gotten to my mother before I could; Ben had been unable to keep the secret to himself; my privacy had been invaded, my trust in Ben abused and my belief in myself shattered.

I could tell my mother was so very disappointed in me. The relationship going public coincided with Daniel's return home, unbeknown to me, as he did not tell me he was coming home, and before I had a chance to talk to him.

The town did what most small rural towns do. The gossips ran riot and I was labelled as undesirable, a sinner in the eyes of the church that I considered my family; unworthy of anything decent in my life; a sinner who had cheated on her boyfriend.

Not surprisingly, Daniel called off the relationship, and I did feel bad for him. I stopped going to church, so I didn't have to walk in with everyone looking at me. It was hard for me to see Beth, Daniel's sister and knowing she knew what I had done. Somehow, I thought that my behaviour would cause Daniel to change his behaviour, cause him to fight for me, but he didn't.

The family on both sides never gave up trying to put us together in the same places at the same time. I was sure, despite what had happened, that Daniel still had deep feelings for me, but he was never actually able to articulate them.

At the tender age of eighteen, I gave up on relationships and opted for short-term associations and one-night stands instead. Looking back, I allowed myself to be used by men. Deep down inside I was, of course, still looking for the man of my dreams, but I was always cast aside for the ex-girlfriend, or the new girl in town, or the prettier girl, or the girl whose parents had more money, or his parents approved of. I accepted it and even expected it in time. It was a recipe for mental health disaster and a series of 'unfortunate' incidents that pushed me even lower.

One evening I was asked to drop a boyfriend's mate home. It resulted in a "date rape", except we never had a date. He pushed me into his house, whilst trying to kiss me and then wouldn't let me leave. However, many times I said 'No' to this 6'2 footballer he wasn't listening and I was overpowered. I'm only 154 centimetres tall and at the time weighted just 46 kilograms. Tiny. He did what he wanted and I couldn't stop him. He played for the local team and was married, so given I had driven him home I felt I couldn't go to the police. I was also too ashamed to tell anyone, believing that it was somehow my fault.

Another time, a man, someone I considered a friend, led me into a toilet block to get away from a group of rowdy youths following behind us. I thought he was being sweet, trying to protect me, but as soon as we were inside he pounced on me. He managed to lock the stall door and I had no way of escape. All the time I expected him to stop when he realised that I was truly not interested, but he didn't.

Another episode occurred when I had a lucky escape. I was asked out to a party and arrived at the appointed time and place to discover that I was the only girl invited, having been dropped by a taxi and knowing there was no quick way home. I remember feeling desperately scared. In the end, I feigned awful stomach pains and managed to run off. It could have been a very nasty situation.

What I needed was not the attention of uncaring strangers, but help, counselling, love, and assistance. But I didn't know that back then. The damage to my soul would just continue with each passing year.

It was during this time, that I realised I might be clinically depressed. I went to see a doctor who I worked with. I was sitting in her office, tears streaming down my face for no reason and she was trying to help. She suggested I might need antidepressants. I didn't know it then, but there was a strong family history of depression. All I knew was that I didn't want to have this diagnosis on my health record. I had visions of being placed in a psychiatric ward and never, ever being let out. Depression was an ugly word back then, so I rejected her offer of a prescription.

Had I listened to her I would have had help earlier, and so much of the damage in my life might have been averted. I didn't realise how the blackness was stealing my vision and impairing my thinking. I know medication and therapy can control depression, but I didn't give myself that luxury. I also didn't have the luxury of good female friends. I was friends with far more men than women. I feared girls my own age would judge me and gossip about me behind my back. I would learn later that men can be far greater gossips than women and less inclined to tell the truth.

I did maintain relationships with the group of girls that I had trained with. Had I actually confided in them, this group of girls could have been a source of great comfort and understanding. Each of them had their own stories to tell and together we could have helped each other through some very tough times.

However, a couple of the partners of these girls did stand up for me one morning after a particularly harrowing experience in the house we all shared. After a party, with a houseful of party goers staying overnight, I was visited by a drunken reveller who would not take "no" for an answer. I had given up my double bedroom upstairs to one of the other couples, and had a mattress on the floor downstairs, towards the back of the house, tucked away in a dark corner so I could sleep without being woken by all the others in the morning. During the night when everyone was asleep, this big guy jumped on top of me and would not get off me. I shouted "stop", "please stop" and "no, I don't want this" but the guy didn't stop, and no one heard me. Certainly, no one came to help.

The next morning, two of the girl's boyfriends asked if I was okay. I burst into tears and explained what had happened. They asked if

I wanted to call the police. I really did not want to get anyone into trouble; I was embarrassed, ashamed and scared of confronting this man in the cold hard light of day. The guys rounded up the offender and made him apologise for his behaviour, explained that they would and could call the police on him if he ever touched me again. They finally made him promise to never attack any other girl again either. I vaguely remember him bleating something about being too drunk to remember, but I knew that he knew what he had done was wrong. I did not know this guy except as a bloke who hung out with a group of guys we went out with sometimes. I was exhausted from lack of sleep, having lain awake after the fact fearing he would return.

In those days in Australia, there was no education about sexual assault or the need to report sexual assault to the police. The balance of the sexes was severely weighted. I have numerous friends who all tell of similar stories of non-consensual sex. One friend who lived in the same town who disclosed to me as many as five rapes, some of them resulting in unplanned pregnancies and subsequent abortions. She did not report any to the police. There was a pervasive culture of secrecy around the issue of rape and sexual assault that existed in the town at that time. We were, well I was, as a woman, conditioned to believe we were at fault in all encounters, simply by virtue of what we were wearing, where we were and how much we'd had to drink.

None of this helped my depression. There were times when the darkness descended like a cloud I couldn't see through; suffocating me, drowning me. I moved into a house with one of my nursing mates and her partner, on Oak Street, in Gymthorpe. This couple proved to be very accepting of me and were a steadying influence at a time when my life was starting to spiral out of control. Many, many years later I would reflect on this couple as being the first people to try to help me with my demons; the first couple to demonstrate what real relationships looked like. This couple would also go on to prove that relationships can go the distance and come out the other side; 30 years later with three kids and still very much in love.

My endless procession of one-night stands in a bid to emulate them continued with a succession of men. But they were doomed from the start as I never felt beautiful or intelligent enough to warrant any more than a fleeting interest. Even though I was regularly having sex outside of marriage, I still believed it was wrong. It was like constantly pressing the self-destruct button.

During my time at the Oak Street house, one of my relationships almost stuck. He was a lovely young man from a stable loving family, with big dreams and amazingly he decided that I was the one for him. We spent lots of quality time together and with his family, planning our future. I loved his mother and felt for the first time that perhaps I might "fit" somewhere. She treated me as a person worthy of being with her son. Spending time with his mother enriched me in a way that few older females had in a long time. But my relationship with James was interrupted by his acceptance into the Air Force. This was a huge thing for a young man from our small rural country town. I was immensely proud of him.

He had to go away for his initial block of training which was a bit of a wrench given we had grown so close.

I went with him and his family to stay the night at his aunt and uncle's house close to the airport, before he was due to fly out the next day. It was a lovely day, but it was punctuated by what I perceived as his grandmother's dislike of me. Up to that point, it appeared everyone in James' family had approved of me, but I felt like this woman didn't, and it brought out my feelings of insecurity in a horrible rush. Whether it was real or imagined, the feeling was compounded by what happened that night, as we readied for bed.

In those days, you might have been living and sleeping with someone but there were places where you just pretended that this was not the case. So as everyone else was shown to a bedroom to sleep, I was taken into a separate room, but there was no bed in it. For a moment I was bewildered, but then I was handed a sheet and a blanket, and it was obvious I was expected to just sleep on the floor.

Since the house was full and there were probably no more beds to be had, I accepted the situation. James had a big day ahead and he at least needed a good night's sleep in a proper bed. Perhaps that is why they had not given his bed to me. I didn't want to make a fuss, so I settled down to sleep on the floor, feeling a little bit upset, but mainly because I wasn't able to share a bed with my beloved James on his last night. I remember James being apologetic about the sleeping situation, but he didn't offer me his bed either.

He did sneak in beside me for a little while but returned to his single bed before anyone was awake. Needless to say, it was one of the longest, coldest nights of sleep in my memory. The next day James left, and by then I had the perception, that I was probably not good enough for his family.

We wrote often and kept up a long-distance love affair, then a letter of unexpected devotion arrived, surprising me with its content. James had written a beautiful letter saying he wanted to get married and asking me to be his wife. The end of my nursing training would coincide with the finish of his training, and we could move in together and start our lives. Instead of the happiness I expected to feel, fear grabbed my throat. I wondered why this wonderful man would want to marry me? And I thought of what his family would think and say when he announced his intention. So, I declined his lovely proposal, we split up and my downward spiral continued. I was truly my own worst enemy.

Years later James and I were able to reconnect on Facebook. He remembered our time together with fondness and has been very happily married himself for more than 30 years. He said that he did not realise how much I was struggling with my emotions at the time, so obviously I was good at hiding them. I have found a reconnection with the past a very healing endeavour, and for the most part those I have spoken to have been very positive and supportive of me. I wish I had recognised and accepted that support at the time.

After the break-up with James, I made another unsuccessful attempt at ending my miserable life. Being a nurse meant I had easy access to the type of medication that could induce permanent sleep. I hoped that by taking enough tablets I would fall asleep and never wake up from the pain that plagued my soul. Fortunately, in hindsight, I didn't take enough to produce the desired effect and I was woken by my Oak Street roommates. I had taken enough sleeping tablets to induce a coma in an elephant, but they did not work on me for whatever reason, thankfully. It was more a cry for help, to end the pain I was feeling and my inability to soothe my soul.

They called my parents and the arrival of my mother compounded my self-loathing. I still refused to admit the obvious, that I had depression, was suicidal and suffering from a deep-seated anxiety disorder. Even if I had admitted to myself that I needed help, getting help and assistance at that time in history would have carried an enormous stigma, so I just got up and got on with things as best I could.

I was two years into my nursing training by then and the next life-changing sequence of events happened quite unexpectedly, but looking back, it was the perfect storm of a life spiralling out of control; a desperation for love, deepening depression and anxiety and still not recognising the difference between sexual attraction and real love.

Every Wednesday night, my nursing mates and I went to the Tattersalls Hotel for cheap drinks, good food, great music and dancing.

I had never really learned how to fit into the Aussie culture of drinking. I wasn't exposed to alcohol prior to leaving home, so found it difficult to judge how much to drink. I drank to fit in, I drank to become uninhibited and to breach the shyness and discomfort I felt around people I did not know well. I drank to be sociable, I drank to smother the pain. I drank to make myself more likable. Alcohol and I were best friends during that time and I could binge drink myself into oblivion.

The hotel was well-known as a meeting place for the young and beautiful intent on a night of revelry. Mind you, there were a few of the not-so-young intent on reliving their youth too. The atmosphere was always charged with excitement and youthful enthusiasm. The music reverberated down the street. This night was no different than any other Wednesday night, except that two dysfunctional young people would be drawn together like moths to a flame, neither knowing how they would go on to impact on each other's lives.

I can still remember everything vividly, some 32 years later. Across the dance floor, I saw the most gorgeous guy I had ever laid eyes on, dressed all in denim, sporting a sandy moustache and messy blond hair, a slim, sexy body with eyes that pierced my soul. Seeing him for the first time set off lightning bolts in my head and tingles down my entire body. I fell instantly in lust. As he made his way towards me, I knew already the result of the night, but had little understanding of the greater role this meeting would play out in my life.

Meet Gerald, father of my daughter, one very fractured but beautiful young man. Having lost his father before he was even aware of his existence, Gerald was raised by a single mother who was very scarred by the accidental death of her husband in a mining disaster in Mount Isa. Gerald was a local ratbag, known for blowing his entire inheritance on a rather stunning black and white hatchback Holden Torana. The fastest car in the district, it was known for its ability to outrun the police. This was a young man living dangerously.

The attraction between us was instant and overpowering for all the wrong reasons. My penchant for self-destruction had just stepped up a notch, as I picked the most reckless young man in the district.

Unbeknown to me that night, Gerald already had a girlfriend. Apparently, everyone knew that night, except me. Not that it would have made a difference, as the attraction between us was so strong. I didn't know Gerald from a bar of soap, but I did recognise electric attraction when I felt it. I would like to think that had I been aware of the existence of a girlfriend it would have stopped the relationship progressing beyond the dance floor. We drank and danced all night, until almost dawn. Little memory remains of what happened between leaving the hotel and the next morning, except to say that I woke up in love, in the bed of a man I hardly knew.

Alarm bells should have registered as soon as I went home with him to his bedroom, at his mother's house! There were loads of boxes in the garage as he parked the car. He said they were his girlfriend's, but when I looked at him quizzically, he changed it to an ex-girlfriend and said she had just left some stuff behind when they split up. If they were no longer together, why were there boxes of her stuff stored in his garage? My alcohol dulled brain failed to make the connection. In the morning his mother looked at me like I had committed a crime, but I had no idea why. It wasn't until a few days later after we had become inseparable, that a childhood friend, Shirley, told me he did indeed have a girlfriend. Gerald insisted they had broken up weeks before and she had gone to live with her sister. In fact, he was two-timing his girlfriend and this was the first of many, many lies he would tell me.

Gerald had abandonment issues which obviously stemmed from the loss of his father when he was a toddler. It made him very needy. Anytime he was left alone for a period of time, like when I was working, he would start drinking excessively and party, often sleeping around. I lost count of the number of times he cheated on me, but I still loved him.

Tumultuous would be an apt description of the relationship between myself and Gerald. We were very much in love, very passionate, very demonstrative, fun-loving and we had loads of adventures. But the good times were tempered with insane, unjustified, outbursts of jealousy, total control, manipulation and lying from Gerald. His temper erupted like Mount Vesuvius at the slightest thing. These jealous fits of rage would turn from verbal to physical, but I tolerated his behaviour because it was always followed by his tears, begging for forgiveness and a promise to never do it again. It was a promise he was never able to keep.

To be fair I knew nothing else, as this was a familiar pattern for me, having seen it over and over in my own family life. I had often seen my mother and father argue and my mother burst into torrents of tears, which generally achieved the end of the argument.

I should have realised the destructive nature of this cycle when he demanded that I burn anything that I owned from any previous relationships. I should have known that his ideas of escaping Gymthorpe were more about isolating me rather than going on any adventure. I should have realised that anyone who stops you spending time with your friends is not someone to have in your life long-term and that anyone who can lie so blatantly is not a good person to be around. I should have known, but I didn't.

I vividly remember him taking my younger brother for a drive at 160 kilometres an hour through the urban streets of Gymthorpe. My brother emerged from the car whiter than a ghost. This was the start of my brother's immense dislike of Gerald a dislike that escalated to a point where he said he wanted to physically harm him.

Gerald wrecked his car and my car and just kept going. His mother scolded him occasionally, but still covered for him if the police came knocking at the door. Gerald was charismatic, charming and demonstrative; all the things I wanted in a man. I just ignored all the bad stuff.

After only six months we were engaged! By that time, we were living together on a rural property in Tamaree, a rural suburb on the outskirts of Gymthorpe. We had started to plan our lives together. He found work requiring him to travel to the nearby town of Maryborough and instead of driving his beaten-up old Land Rover, or the Torana which was kept in perfect condition in the shed, he wanted to drive my little car. I was left with the problematic, difficult to start Land Rover. Our lives were plagued with difficulties from lack of money to broken down vehicles, to all sorts of things going wrong. On the night of our engagement party, I ended up in the hospital with unexplained abdominal pain and a raging fever. The universe was trying to tell me something and I wasn't listening. We had no plans to get married immediately so maybe some part of me was protecting myself, even then.

When my nursing training was successfully over the big wide world beckoned. Gerald and I packed up our two dogs, a small caravan, the four-wheel drive and headed for the great prospects of Mount Isa. Mount Isa was a large mining town located in the middle of Western Outback Queensland- a 19-hour drive from Gymthorpe without stops. The mining company that his father had worked for had promised Gerald a job if ever he made it back to Mount Isa. I started working at the Mount Isa Base Hospital. We lived in a dodgy caravan park where we survived on bread and Vegemite sandwiches, barely enough room to sleep, no air-conditioning in the summer heat in Mount Isa and with two little dogs to keep us company. It was a brutal, raw place and so were the people.

One night after a late shift, I had a maniac jump into the shower with me.

I can attest that it is true that your brain moves in slow motion when you are in danger. I could see a man trying to climb into the shower cubicle, but my brain did not compute what was happening. I remember thinking it was one of Gerald's friend's playing a prank and then quickly realised it was not a prank. To this day, almost 31 years later, I can still see his piercingly blue, soulless eyes, intent on getting to me like a wolf with its prey. I screamed the loudest scream I had ever emitted, and it saved me. He took off and I stood shaking, naked and wet in the shower. Finally, I dried myself off and went outside, where a nearby family asked if I was okay. I collapsed to the ground crying and the police were summoned immediately. Even though there was a search, the man was never found. I no longer felt safe in that caravan park, but there was nowhere else to go so we stayed.

At the Mount Isa Base hospital, I fell in with a group of lovely young girls who all socialised together. We took turns meeting up at each other's places and went on outings together. It was this group of older girls who first started to point out to me how wrong Gerald's behaviour was and how it was impacting on my life. Little did I know that the worst was yet to come, and I would be grateful for their wise words and kind encouragement.

Our lives in Mount Isa settled into a bit of a routine of shift work, partying and making friends. Once we had moved to Mount Isa many fellow Gymthorpe locals followed, and Mount Isa began to feel a little like home. One of Gerald's friends moved into a bigger caravan with us and we were able to split the rent. Living accommodation was a little crowded and I hated the lack of privacy, but Byron was a good bloke. He was a good friend, not only to Gerald but to me too, but that was the cause of the next terrifying incident in my life.

The three of us were out one-night drinking yet again at a bar. A man came up to talk to Byron and I, while Gerald was talking to some of his other mates a short distance from us. The next thing I knew, an enraged Gerald was accusing me of flirting with the unknown stranger. Byron tried to stand up for me but Gerald only grew more enraged. I was dragged out of the bar by Gerald, my shoes falling off my feet as he was manhandling me so roughly. I tried to protest and go back for them, but he ignored me. We were followed closely by Byron. I did not even have time to put down the drink I was sipping. Once we were all in Gerald's car, he grabbed the glass I was holding and smashed it into my face, cutting my lower lip. Then he drove off despite being well over the legal limit.

Byron shouted at Gerald to take me to a hospital, as blood was pouring from my lip, but Gerald pushed Byron from the moving vehicle and slammed the door on my arm as I tried to escape too. I was now pleading for him to stop and let me out. Finally, he did, in a paddock outside of town. I remember how dry the sand felt on my bare feet, the Spinifex pricking at my toes and scratching my legs. I started running for my life, not sure where I was or how I would get back to town. The bright lights of Gerald's car began to bear down on me as he gave chase. It felt like I was in a horror movie.

As the lights got closer, Gerald started screaming at me, telling me to run as if it was a game. My brain went into slow motion. He started shouting that he was going to kill me. That was enough to shock my body into action and I ran barefoot through the Spinifex and sand, falling and tripping and scraping my knees and hands, shaking and crying alternately begging for my life, screaming for help, but no one came. Then the vehicle was right behind me and I dodged it as it roared by. To this day I have no idea how I escaped its path.

I dived behind a huge clump of desert grass and hoped that he would not see me. In the distance, I could see some sort of building. It was completely dark, but I could see the faint outline of the building. I thought if I could make it there, I might be safe. I was lying low to the ground, looking for an opportunity to make a run for it. I was too scared to break my cover and I sat in my hiding place for what seemed like hours as Gerald was driving around and around in circles looking for me. How he did not spot me I do not know. Eventually, I got up and made a run for it as soon as I saw the red lights of the back of the vehicle. I made it to the building and hid behind a post and a partial wall, just as the lights of high beam passed over the spot where I had been hiding. I thought that my heart would explode out of my chest it was beating so hard. I was freezing and I hurt from all the cuts and scrapes. Blood was still oozing from my lip. I was shaking with shock, begging silently for someone to help me. Each time the lights of the truck shone in the direction of the building, I stopped breathing, desperately hoping he wouldn't see me.

I lost all concept of time. I didn't know how long I had sheltered behind that wall, in that dilapidated old building. I could feel blood dripping down my legs. I could still taste the blood in my mouth, which had swollen painfully by now. My shoulder hurt from being yanked into the car and my hip ached where the speeding vehicle had brushed too close to me. My teeth were chattering in the cold night air and I struggled to quiet them for fear he would hear. My hands smarted from gravel rash and still I waited and waited. After what seemed like an eternity, the vehicle disappeared. Then, when he had been out of sight for some minutes I screamed out for help, but there was no one there, of course. I slowly started to move from my hiding spot. My feet were frozen, and I am sure I looked hideous. I slowly started walking in the direction of the faint arc of light which I thought was town, hoping that no one would see me. I was ashamed; ashamed that I had trusted this man and put myself in this situation. I did take a moment to look towards the heavens and thank whoever had protected me that night.

A little while later I saw the lights of a vehicle coming towards me and I was so scared that he was coming back for me. I hid just off the road, ready to run again. Gerald had indeed returned, but this time he was driving slowly and calling my name, pleading with me to come out. He said he wanted to take me home, that he was so, so sorry for his actions, and he was crying. In the end, his tears got the better of me and I allowed him to see where I was and drive over to me. He got out of the car, lifted me gently back into it, and held my hand while pleading for my forgiveness. I was twenty; I was ashamed; I had nowhere else to go but home with him.

When I rang my family and told them what had happened, obviously in some distress, they wanted me to return home immediately. But I wasn't one to run away. I thought that I had made my bed and now I had to lie in it. Knowledge and understanding of domestic violence were pretty much zero at that time and no one spoke of the abuse cycle. People would later ask why I didn't leave, but there were so many reasons. I loved him. I thought he could and would change. I believed his lies and trusted what he said. After all, I'd been conditioned to believe him, hadn't I?

The fallout of this episode had an immediate positive effect on Gerald. For a while at least, I was treated like his princess and we did everything I wanted to do. This did not address the reason behind his behaviour, but it mollified me. I forgave him that night because that is what abused victims do and I had become a victim, not just that night but in the episodes and the years leading up to that point. I was not compassionate to myself in anyway.

Not long after this incident, I discovered that I was pregnant. It was unexpected as I was on the pill. Life had dealt me yet another challenge. I now felt there was no option for me but to stay and try to make our relationship work. I owed the father of my child that much, I thought. I really wanted to get married to legitimise this child but there was no way that we could afford it, so I resigned myself to the fact that I was going to be an unmarried mother, at least temporarily. I did not like the idea.

I loved being pregnant. I adored having an excuse for a belly. I didn't enjoy the all-day morning sickness, but I hoped that it would abate in the end. Gerald endlessly expressed his delight at becoming a father. He dreamed of owning his own business and providing a life of luxury for us both. We would have a little farm and we would breed dogs, he told me. "We will be so very happy together", he said. Gerald talked to my belly, telling the baby just how much he loved it and how very wanted this baby was. He wanted a boy and it didn't enter his mind that we might have a girl. We picked out baby names and planned how life would be. What I didn't consider was that he had not had a father, so he had no barometer by which to measure how to be a father. We were both so incredibly young and so unknowing.

At about five months pregnant, Gerald was still drinking and partying, but I could no longer party along with him. So, I played the dutiful wife and stayed at home, waiting up for him to return. There were so many nights when he did not return until very late, or not until the next morning. I suspected he was cavorting with other girls and it made me ill with worry; worry about what the future held for our unborn child and what on earth I was going to do. I had seen this behaviour all my life. My mother had stayed through so many instances of bad behaviour. I thought I should too. Now I know no one should ever put up with that type of behaviour. I would advise others to speak out, not suffer in silence and be brave. I wasn't yet brave, but I would be!

Towards the end of the pregnancy, I was under great pressure from my family to return home to Gymthorpe to have the baby. It was the first grandchild and the first great-grandchild. I wanted to have the baby in Mount Isa; wanted Gerald to be part of that process, but eventually, we decided that I would go home for an extended visit and that Gerald would book holidays and come home in time for the birth of the baby. Well, babies have calendars of their own and this little darling decided to arrive two weeks early, throwing everyone's plans into disarray. This would have a lasting effect on both of us. I was resentful that he didn't make it, and he was resentful that I was in Gymthorpe and not Mount Isa. He arrived the night after her birth and even though she was not the boy he wanted, he was in awe when he held her, so tiny and so perfect, for the first time.

It was a difficult birth. I was in labour for three days; three days, where my doctor was not sure I would stay in actual labour. But then my waters were broken artificially, and the baby was finally delivered eight hours later, I was totally exhausted and numb. There was no instant bond between the baby and me. Here was the most exquisitely beautiful baby girl and I wasn't sure how to feel. I remember my doctor holding her in his arms, marvelling at her tiny toes and feet, delighting in her baby beauty. It was 2.30pm on Saturday the 14th of January 1989 and I was just 21 years old.

This beautiful baby girl remained nameless for several days. There was huge parental pressure from my mother to leave Gerald's surname off the birth certificate and to just have my name and surname. My mother reasoned that it was a simple change when we got married, and in my foggy post-birth brain, I just did what was suggested. There was no conscious thought around it. I have regretted this decision all my life for not only did it deny my daughter her rightful heritage in writing. It caused unnecessary pain to both of them, just to keep the peace.

I had bad tearing requiring numerous stitches and remained in the hospital for a week. The hospital treated me like family and they spoiled me with their care in the maternity ward. When I went home to my parent's place, they refused to let Gerald stay with the baby and me. I can understand their reasons, because we were unmarried, and they simply did not like him. It did not help us strengthen the relationship between the three of us, though. I wasn't bonding with my baby and Gerald wasn't bonding with her either. Finally, it was time to leave and a fractured, hurting little threesome headed home to Mount Isa.

I have no recollection of the trip home apart from ten hours of a screaming baby. Back in Mount Isa, I felt isolated and alone. Our newborn daughter was difficult to feed and screamed day and night. Gerald was little help, and my isolation and depression deepened to the point where I was barely coping. The sleep deprivation and constant screaming of a baby were exhausting. Endless visits to the doctor failed to diagnose what I now think was severe reflux. I wanted my mother to come for a visit, but she said she had too many other things that were demanding her attention. I needed a break, I needed help and there was no one to help in Mount Isa, so reluctantly, when our daughter was three months old, I returned to Gymthorpe. I reasoned Gerald could also get some much-needed sleep. The plan was always to return to Mount Isa when I was better able to settle the baby. It was never expected to be the long-term separation it turned out to be.

When my daughter was about five months old, and we had been back at my parent's place for a couple of months, Daniel's brother Reggie came over for dinner. He was unusually quiet throughout dinner as I babbled on about how well Gerald was doing in Mount Isa. This was unusual for him. He liked to talk, and usually engaged in conversation, but not this evening. When it was time for him to go, I walked him to his car and asked if there was anything wrong. He looked me in the eye and said: "There's something you need to know, and I don't want to tell you, but someone has to."

He explained that not long after I'd had the baby, he and Gerald had gone out to celebrate the birth of our daughter and Gerald had slept with someone else. He also said Gerald had been living with a 17-year-old girl in Mount Isa. It seemed that all this time, when he had been talking to me daily on the phone, telling me he loved me and couldn't wait for us to all be to together again, he was sleeping with a 17-year-old in our house; the house we had moved into in preparation for the birth of our baby. The world crashed in on me as his words reverberated around my head.

"No, that's just not true," I stammered, but I knew it was. I knew that Reggie had been with Gerald that night, and I knew it was the truth. I thought I would die with the grief and pain I felt at that moment. I had put all my trust in this man. We had a child together. I was devastated and I sat on the steps numb with grief. It hurt like no other pain I had experienced before. I wanted to die. I also wanted to kill him and hurt the girl responsible.

I called Gerald. I wanted to get him to admit the truth to me. He denied it all for the longest time and then finally admitted it all, only to state that "I deserved it", as I had left him alone in Mount Isa. What was he expected to do, he asked me? Two deeply flawed young adults inflicted on each other a level of pain that was unbearable. He got to go on living and having fun and I now had to raise a baby by myself.

Neither of my parents placed any importance on my intense grief. For them, it was a blessing and relief that this disastrous relationship was over. That didn't help me at all. I had given my all to be with this man and I loved him absolutely. I was devastated and barely functioned for months. I was a non-attentive mother. I failed to comfort my baby. I wandered around the house aimlessly, mostly in tears trying to deal with my grief. I was exhausted and so worried about the future. I was an unmarried single parent and so very ashamed of who I had become. I should have sought counselling but instead of proper counselling, I talked to a church "pastor" which proved more alienating than helpful. He only emphasised the stigma of single parenthood.

I was so angry with the girl who had slept with Gerald. I went to the car park of her workplace one morning and waited for her to arrive.

As soon as she saw me getting out of the car, she tried to avoid me, but I walked up to her and said, "I know what you did". I was seething; barely keeping a lid on my anger, my fists clenched in rage. I wanted to hit her; pound her to a pulp, but I didn't. She burst into tears then, great big sobs of anguish, and in that instant, I forgave her. I felt myself deflating. I have often wanted to ask her as her own children were born, how she would have felt if someone had done that to her.

I felt like I bore all the shame of our failed relationship. Gerald was off enjoying a new life, with a newer, younger version of myself. Is that even possible at 22 years old? He had a great job; he kept all the furniture we had so carefully gathered together and I was left holding the baby, quite literally.

I thought that perhaps if I got my smile "fixed", life would somehow be better and I would become more desirable. I went back to the doctor who had delivered my baby girl and discussed what could be done with my face. He thought that some new nerve grafting procedure might be helpful and referred me to a neurosurgeon in Brisbane. My father agreed to accompany me and as we left Central Station, I saw a tall, blond man with a briefcase striding up the street ahead of us. I knew instantly that it was Andrew. I called his name, but my words were lost in the crowded street and he did not hear me. I started to hurry after him but could not catch up. I called his name again but to no avail, I could not catch him in the crowded street and he disappeared out of my sight. I was so disappointed, but that little voice in the back of my head reminded me that I was a single mother now and what good would catching up with him be anyway. I was tainted, not good enough, undeserving of even talking to him. Wearily, I continued on my way to the appointment.

I felt at this time that if I could just find someone to marry me then I would be "legitimate" in the eyes of the world. It is that stigma which continues to this day, even in these more enlightened times. The word 'single' emanates failure, as if a judgment is required when what is really required is help and support to strengthen the next generation. My family also made it clear I was obliged to remarry so they too could hold their heads up high. It was a huge amount of responsibility on such fragile shoulders.

Suddenly, Daniel re-entered my life. He was back in town for a visit to see family and friends. Given he was my mother's choice of husband for me, I thought I should take another look. I realised I had hardly given him a chance before. A long-distance relationship had not been for me earlier in my life but perhaps he was the escape route out of Gymthorpe now.

He came over to my parents' house to visit them and to meet baby Courtney. She seemed to like him, as much as a six-month-old can. We talked on and off, most of the afternoon and I could see that he was still very interested in me. I was reminded of his hard-working ethics and his quiet, gentle nature. There were no fireworks, just a realisation that he felt generous and good. He was going back to the mining town of Blackwater and he suggested that we keep in contact. It felt good to be liked by someone again.

I organised trips up to Blackwater to see and stay with him and over time we grew closer. I thought I loved him enough to make a life with him after all. He gave me a sense of acceptance and I longed to be accepted. He could give legitimacy to my daughter and we might even be able to have more children. I did not allow myself the luxury of being over Gerald. I just needed a solution. In five months, we were engaged, and we planned to be married six weeks after that. We were on a collision course to disaster!

My school friend Shirley came to visit again and begged me not to marry Daniel. Shirley knew how passionately I had loved Gerald and could not see the same passion in me for Daniel. I tried to explain that I was doing what was best for my daughter; that Daniel and I were good friends and that we would be able to make it work. She reminded me why I had walked away from the relationship before, insisting that there needed to be something more than a friendship to make it in the long term.

I told her I thought it was all too late anyway, as the marriage was arranged and everything had been organised. I knew I couldn't back out now and disappoint my parents, even if I was unsure of my feelings. One thing I was certain of was that Daniel could be a good father to Courtney. That mattered more than anything I was feeling unsure about.

Her parting words, however, would haunt me years later: "Don't do this. He's not right for you and you'll be sorry. I don't want to see you hurt again".

Her words, of course, played on my mind all the way up to the wedding day. I told myself I was doing the right thing but deep down inside of me I knew it wasn't. I was settling for something less than I deserved. While walking down the front steps of my parents' home towards my future husband, waiting below, I dared to tell my father I thought I couldn't go through with it.

"Get down those bloody steps" – was his only reply and my fate was sealed.

Looking back now, it is easy to see that convention was at the root of all my poor decisions; ignoring my intuition and satisfying social mores. It seems daft now to think that I was so desperate for a partner when I was more than strong enough to raise my daughter alone.

In my mind, married life was supposed to be a loving picture of romance and connection; of a couple working together to make a life for themselves and their little family; of shared ideals, shared dreams and common threads of life experience. This marriage was not like that at all and six weeks in I knew I had made a huge mistake. I was married but lonely; deeply craving physical intimacy and emotional connection.

I did love him, but I had married what I already knew – a relationship plagued with issues, arguments, lacking in physical touch and devoid of any deeper level of communication and understanding.

He just did not talk; did not express the love he purportedly felt for me. He told others how he felt but was generally a man of very few words at home. I didn't realise at that stage, that he didn't know how to communicate. Others told me though that I was the girl he had wanted all his life and now he had me, he did not know what to do with me. He started drinking and working longer and longer hours. I thought he was avoiding me so, the 23-year-old me decided that a baby might help and heal us.

Our first attempt at having a baby ended in heartbreak with a miscarriage. For all the women who have ever endured the pain of the loss of a much-wanted baby, you will know how much it hurts. The pain never leaves you. The memory of the loss leaves a scar on your heart that heals over eventually but is never forgotten. I really, really wanted the baby and I blamed myself for not being able to carry it to term.

To heal that hurt, we got a little black kitten. Of course, an animal cannot replace a baby, but it did help ease some of the pain. Courtney loved the kitten and it kept her entertained for hours and brought the both of us loads of laughter. That was until a drunken incident ended its poor little life. I was busy upstairs readying the toddler for dinner when I heard a screech of tires. After an afternoon of drinking, Daniel had decided to move the car and had run over the kitten. I could not forgive him for his carelessness. There were many of these little hurts in our married life and they just seemed to reinforce the hopelessness. Had I had the knowledge and understanding to seek assistance for both of us, we may have stood some chance of having a healthy relationship. But I thought seeking assistance was a sign of failure; now I know it is a sign of emotional maturity.

When I was about four months pregnant for the third time, the three of us moved from Gymthorpe to Blackwater so that Daniel could obtain a better-paid job in mining. Blackwater was a "backwater"; a small mining town where there was little to do and not much to keep people occupied. Here we socialised with one couple on a regular basis. They were originally friends of Daniel, who became my friends as well. Diana and Brett tried to help with our obviously failing marriage by giving advice and support but could only do so much.

This pregnancy was different from my first and second. Although I did not suffer from the all-day morning sickness of the previous pregnancies, I was more tired and a lot bigger, earlier than expected. After a regular visit to my doctor for an ultrasound at 28 weeks pregnant, he expressed concern about the amount of fluid surrounding the baby. I was given a referral to a specialist, two hours away in Rockhampton and told to make my way there urgently. Panic gripped my heart. Had the move been too much for the pregnancy? Had I harmed the baby in some way? I was always blaming myself when there was no blame to be laid.

It was the Thursday before the Easter break of 1991 and we were supposed to be going off camping with a group of workmates and friends. I thought I would just get a check-up by the specialist and then we could still enjoy the weekend camping. Sitting in the obstetrician's office we were stunned to find that I had a condition called Polyhydramnios, which meant that there was too much amniotic fluid surrounding the baby and it would probably cause a premature birth. The specialist insisted that I go into hospital for bed rest until the baby was delivered. It was the last thing I wanted to do. So that Easter I was stuck in the hospital while my husband and daughter went camping. I cried for 24 hours straight, taking myself off to the shower so no one would hear me sobbing.

I was terrified for the baby and missing my toddler. I felt so alone. It was all so unexpected. I didn't have the baby room prepared, or the toddler toilet-trained yet. They said I couldn't go home to Blackwater as I would be two hours away from specialist obstetric services, so I had to rely on others to care for my daughter whilst my husband continued to work.

For the next six weeks, I tried to stave off premature labour. Each time labour started, it would stop by itself, or they gave me drugs to stop the labour progressing. My target was thirty-eight weeks so that the baby would be mature enough to survive. I was also given injections to help mature the baby's lungs because no one expected the pregnancy to last that long. Thankfully, I wasn't told about all the things that could go wrong, or I would have worried even more.

It was too far for my husband and daughter to travel frequently to see me, so, for the most part, I was alone except for a few cherished visitors. One of my nursing mates drove from Bundaberg to Rockhampton to take me out to lunch, another beloved uncle and auntie drove up from Gladstone each weekend to take me out too. I lived for their visits and will never forget the loving kindness they showed me during that time. Finally, my Mum came to visit, and this coincided with pre-term labour that wasn't stopping. I was thirty-five and a half weeks pregnant.

The morning of the birth of my son is indelibly etched into my memory. I was awoken by the familiar pang of labour pains, but these were more intense and closer together than those that I had previously. At about 7.30 in the morning, just as staff changeover was happening, I felt a trickle of fluid that quickly escalated to a huge gush of amniotic fluid. It quickly saturated the entire bed, splashed onto the floor and spread out into a pool around the bed. As soon as the first midwife appeared, I could see the concern written all over her face. The baby monitor alarm started to sound and more staff arrived. Suddenly the foetal heart rate on the monitor dipped to just 20 beats per minute. It should normally be about 140 beats per minute. The midwife raced to examine me only to discover the baby's cord was hanging out of me. She pushed the cord back up inside and held the baby in while she yelled for the doctor, who had just arrived on the floor.

I was going into shock and the baby was fighting for its little life. Simultaneously I had two drips inserted and a catheter, all whilst the baby was being held inside me, the midwife's hand now replaced by the obstetrician's. I was raced to the operating theatre. I remember hearing that the baby's heart rate was dipping again and as my own was rapidly increasing. I was prepped and draped, still with a hand inside me. As the anaesthetist started to drift me off to sleep I heard him say: "Stay close nurse, this one's going to be a difficult one". The descending blackness stilled the blind panic I felt in my heart. I wanted my husband.

My son was born via emergency caesarean section at 8am on Friday the 10th May 1991. He was five and a half weeks early and weighed just 5lb 2oz or 2.3kg. I wish the staff had waited for me to be awake to have the first cuddle of my son, but instead, my mother got to hold him before I did. It took his father until lunchtime to arrive at the hospital; another missed birth by the father of my baby.

I woke from the general anaesthetic about 10.30 am to find myself alone in my room and desperately worried about the baby. I didn't even know if he was okay. Finally, a nurse arrived to explain that he was safely in a humidicrib in the neonatal intensive care unit, where he would be monitored for a few days. He was perfectly okay, she said, just needing oxygen for a while. All the abnormalities that had had the team so concerned before his birth were not evident in any way. He was perfect, just tiny. When I cradled him in my arms that day, I was in love. I felt overwhelmed by a motherly bonding, which I had not experienced with my daughter until she was much older. It was amazing, but then I felt guilty for feeling this way about him and when I had not felt that way about my daughter when she was born.

It was wonderful to get back home, but life with two little ones was busy. There was little time for anything but the workload of raising small children. Thankfully my son slept through the night from just six weeks old, a feat his sister failed to accomplish until she was sixteen months old. He seemed to be growing exponentially fast to make up for his early entry into the world. His only health issues were with his middle ear infections. This was solved with the removal of his adenoids and insertion of grommets at an early age. I was very focused on the children, which is probably lucky because by this stage my husband and I were hardly talking at all and we had no sex life whatsoever.

When the children were three and a half and eighteen months old, a business opportunity in Gymthorpe presented itself. Daniel and I would partner with my parents in a commercial distributing company, selling packaging and cleaning products directly to other businesses. It would mean that we would be back closer to family, but we would also be working for the future of our little family. I thought that it might just be the shake-up our marriage needed. So, we packed up and moved back to Gymthorpe to start a new life with a business.

I went from being a stay at home mum to working full time in the space of a few weeks and I hated it. I loved the business but hated being away from my kids. It is the bane of working mums world over. Working is engaging, and you get to have adult time away from the kids, but you miss your children immensely and I was no different from most other working mums.

I tried everything I could to make things work and still, they did not. Daniel refused to join me at couple's counselling. I did not know how to walk away. I had already failed before in my relationship with Gerald and failure again was not an option. I felt trapped in a loveless marriage, but I didn't want to be a single mother again. I didn't want my kids to grow up as part of a broken family. I knew the statistics and I knew how badly a broken home could affect a child, however young, but so could growing up in a tense, loveless union.

I had started a platonic friendship with one of the local transport drivers who delivered to our business. He was so nice to me and seemed willing to talk about anything and everything. In my fractured dysfunctional life, he offered the light of friendship. There were so many dysfunctional relationships around me. I had a friend who was seeing a married man; another friend struggling with being gay although he did not know it at the time; friends with broken marriages; friends in abusive relationships. I had no barometer of normal at the time. In this environment, I decided to have a 28th birthday party. Why not add alcohol to this dysfunctional group and see what happens, I thought?

The night was a lovely balmy April evening under the stars. I had invited everyone I knew, and they all came; lots of people, kids, and fun. As the night wore on Daniel proceeded to drink himself into oblivion. At one stage our son tried to get his attention and received a backhand across the face for his efforts. It was the last straw for me. As I put the children to bed, cradling my sobbing son in my arms, I knew that things could not continue as they were.

After settling the children, I rejoined the party, intent on drinking away my pain. I spent the night chatting with friends and mostly enjoying the attentive company of Brendan the "transport driver". By this stage, Daniel was comatose upstairs. I ended up sitting on Brendan's knee. It was just a bit of fun amongst friends at first, but then I heard him whisper: "Let's get out of here", and I went. Looking back now, I have no idea what I was thinking, but I followed him, lured by the promise of something better; romance, love, affection, all the things I craved. What an illusion it all was. That one night ended my marriage. I had transgressed and could not go back. The next morning, I told Daniel it was over. We had been married four years.

The fallout was immediate and traumatic. By the time a woman gets to the point where she either has a one-night stand or an affair, she has mentally left the marriage anyway. I bore the full blame from not only his family but my family as well. It felt like they all sided with Daniel. The small-town gossips had a field day. I knew it took two to tango and I had begged Daniel for years to get help, but all the reasoning in the world was redundant. In my mind there was no use going back, whatever the consequences.

The business became the first casualty. Daniel and I could obviously not continue working together, so he and I and my parents decided to sell up. When the business was sold I went back to being a stay at home mother. It seemed to make sense to get back into nursing, but to regain my registration licence and gain employment, I had to do a 're-entry to nursing course' over a year, because I had not nursed in five years. So now I was not only an unemployed single mother, I was back in school.

The years that followed were again marred by a series of short-lived relationships and one-night stands. This lifestyle only cemented my worthlessness in my own eyes.

My advice to anyone is, if you are going to live a self-destructive life, don't do it in a small town where everybody knows everybody else and nobody can keep a secret. Brendan became a regular on my playlist, but he had no commitment or desire to make the relationship public or permanent. He broke my heart again and again. I put up with his bad behaviour even though the relationship was far from satisfying because I thought that just maybe he would change his mind and discover I was the one for him. I thought that if I was there for him often enough, I stood a chance of being in a relationship with him permanently. Instead, one day he told me that because his parents were so rich, he had to choose a partner wisely, and I was a single mother and therefore not worthy to be his wife. I suspected that he would find his 'pretty young thing', marry her and have a couple of kids. She would then discover that all his money did not compensate for his lack of emotional depth and she would leave, take his money and find happiness elsewhere. Funnily enough, this is exactly what came to pass.

Other unsuitable relationships followed Brendan. There was one who arrived at ungodly hours and left before the kids awoke. His mother worked at the local childcare centre. I made a simple, meaningless comment to her one day saying, "I bet you're glad he's home this week". She turned to me and said in no uncertain terms that I was to "stay away from her son" and that I "wasn't good enough to even have a friendship with him". I cried all the way home. The "me" today looks at the "me" back then and wants to scream: "Don't let her talk to you that way, she has no right". Nobody has any right to judge anyone or make assumptions or be mean and hurtful. No one!! Her comments make me angry even today. How dare she!

During this time there was a high school reunion. The prospect of seeing Andrew again after all that time filled me with excited anticipation. It was always interesting to see what people had done with their lives, but it was a huge disappointment as Andrew was apparently overseas in Europe and could not attend.

I was so dejected, I wished that I had the courage to call in on his parents on my way home, but my insecurity saw me drive up to the property and quickly turn around and drive away, not knowing if they would welcome a divorced mother of two. I should have known that it would never have been a problem and a cup of tea with them and it may have soothed some of the disappointment I was feeling that weekend.

Chapter

Threatening Thirties

"There are wounds that never show on the body that are deeper and more hurtful than anything that bleeds." LAURELL K. HAMILTON

I remember the lead-up to turning thirty years old. It was a powerfully turbulent time for me. The questions in my brain went round and round and round in my head with seemingly no resolution. I did not want to be thirty, unmarried, unsettled and without the prospect of further children. I had always wanted 3 children, but it was looking increasingly like that was never going to happen. I struggled with what I was and what I had become; what I had not achieved in life became painfully obvious and I was plagued with weight issues and low self-esteem. I had a "turning 30" crisis!

I have since learnt that for women, turning thirty can be one of the most transitional times of their lives and is considered a first "rite of passage" into adulthood. It is a time when we redefine our values and priorities. It's a period which usually lasts two to three years. I had the misconception that I would have everything figured out by thirty and it made me anxious and insecure about life in general. As I entered this transitional time, I was yet to discover the difference between working hard on a relationship with someone you love and trying too hard to push an outcome that was not right for me.

What I learned in my thirties was simply to recognise that the voice inside my head is not always my own. Sometimes that voice was my mum's, or my sister's, or my ex's or society's. And often it does not really know ME at all. So I realised that I didn't have to listen to all those other voices. I only needed to listen to the one voice that I know is clearly mine: the forgiving, loving, creative, generous, nurturing voice that only wants what is best for me. She's lovely. I encourage you to do the same.

As I turned thirty, I met a girl whose son also went to the same childcare centre as Billy. We became friends and once she knew I was single, she asked me around to dinner at her place to meet her brother. We had a lovely dinner and conversation flowed freely. I saw Greg as a broken man, who had been through a lot. We hit it off, but I knew after our first night together that something wasn't quite right. I should have cut my losses and run, but I thought I could "fix" him. I was so wrong.

The early part of our relationship was quite good, and we spent time socialising and meeting people that he knew. Many of my friends already knew Greg and this made going out to dinner fun. Greg was gentlemanly enough to open doors for me and send me flowers. He was a talker and there was no end of conversations about everything from growing up to religion. Greg was very opinionated and I liked his strong character. He was readily affectionate and liked to "show me off" around town.

About six months into the relationship the children and I moved onto Greg's 5-acre property and home, about 10 minutes outside of Gymthorpe. It was a wonderful property with a lovely home built on the rise of a hill overlooking farmland. I loved it, the kids loved it, but I knew it would never be "ours".

Early in the relationship I had made a promise to not make any claims on his property if we were to split up at any stage. In return, he promised to not make any claim on my house in town. Not long after we started dating, my divorce from Daniel was finalised, with me retaining ownership of my house in town and sharing custody of both children.

Even though it was essentially Greg's home, I worked hard on the gardens and spent many, many weekends mowing the wonderful big lawn. The kids loved the fresh air and countryside to run around on and they rode their bikes from morning until evening. It was pretty much idyllic when we were there by ourselves. Greg worked very long hours, six to seven days a week and if he wasn't working, he was sleeping, so the kids and I had a lot of time to enjoy the country setting on our own.

Greg loved company and was always organising a gathering of friends and family when he was off work. He was a great social entertainer and we had so many fun-filled evenings. In a social setting he was a master of ceremonies, adept at holding court with many and a great story teller. However, these wonderful qualities did not make up for his anger issues, or his verbal tirades.

Greg had had a failed marriage which haunted him. He had started a relationship with a high school student when he was in his late twenties, which I must admit worried me a little. Eventually Kayley and Greg had married, by which time he was in business with another guy running a milk tanker business. He told me that Kayley and his business partner had had an affair and that Kayley had gotten pregnant by his partner, although there was a part of him that also believed that the baby was his. Greg ended the marriage, but never got over the betrayal and the heartbreak and it reared its head in frequent anger, and sometimes blatant disrespect for women. At least I knew this feeling: there was some comfort in familiarity.

Greg was also soliciting close relationships with other women, or rather girls, while he was with me. He believed that he was not being unfaithful unless he slept with them. I learnt that he often had young girls in his truck on the pretext of befriending them and teaching them about life. It seemed sordid behaviour and our arguments were ferocious. Again, I was desperate for his love and attention and expected if I kept loving him the best that I could, he would one day love me as I wanted him to. But he was unable to give that to me.

The children were scared of him and it took the innocence of my children to break me out of Greg's spell.

One day, I studied my son and daughter, sitting opposite me at the kitchen table. The pair had become increasingly difficult to manage and had been causing problems at school as well as at home. At ten and eight years of age, respectively, life had handed them a lot to cope with, but I had always expected them to behave as responsible and reasonable children. I never allowed them to use their "single parent upbringing", or the "from a broken family" or "we have a step parent" tags as an excuse for anything other than an acknowledgement that these elements were part of the fabric of their lives. Looking back, I was perhaps expecting too much of two such young children living through such a turbulent home life.

That day I asked them: "What's going on with you guys? You have never been this badly behaved before, and your behaviour in the last six months has been appalling. What on earth is the matter?" They both looked at each other and then burst into tears.

"We're afraid that Greg is going to kill you; we're scared, and we want you to leave," said my daughter.

At that moment I was stunned, but then I leapt to my feet and grabbed them both in a bear hug. It was not possible to feel more ashamed than I did right then. I had naively thought that by providing a wonderful place for them to live, being a loving Mum and shielding them from the violent outbursts of my partner, I had given them a good solid base. Clearly, I was very wrong.

With tears dried and little emotions placated for the time being, the children went on to tell me exactly what they had been feeling in the previous months. They described how they would hide under their beds during arguments, hoping that they and I would be safe, they said they had plotted how they would run away and then come back and rescue me. I felt like crawling into a hole, but I knew then how my relationship was impacting on the most precious little people in my world. Greg was a good provider and could be loving and playful, but there was a dark side to him.

I had to accept that I had failed at another relationship. Years later, I was able to see that the relationship had been doomed from the beginning, and I was simply following a familiar pattern. It took hindsight to recognise this.

At about the same time as my breakup with Greg, my sister decided to move to Brisbane. I decided I would do the same thing and get out of Gymthorpe.

In between ending the relationship with Greg and moving to Brisbane, I went to a Christmas party. A few drinks and a few dances would lead to the most soul destroying, deeply traumatic relationship of them all.

TONI LONTIS

Chapter

Predatory Man

"We mute the realization of malevolence- which is too threatening to bear - by turning offenders into victims themselves and by describing their behavior as the result of forces beyond their control." ANNA SALTER, PREDATORS: PAEDOPHILES, RAPISTS, AND OTHER SEX OFFENDERS

Aamon exuded a charisma that lured me in. He was relatively good looking, with dark hair, a slim body and tanned skin. He had the ability to spin a good story, but I noticed that he did seem to deflect any deeper questioning. He preferred to talk about me, he said, and he remembered everything I said and repeated it back to me. He made me feel like he was listening and understanding what I said. He made me feel safe.

He knew Greg and said that he knew Greg was entertaining very young girls in his truck and that everyone who worked at the transport company had known about it too. Shame no one had discussed it with me sooner than they did. Aamon seemed to have empathy for me and he made me feel less of a fool for not acting earlier.

Aamon was a great dancer and I found this quality alluring, as Greg had never ever wanted to dance in public with me. Aamon was also a gentleman, opening doors, pulling out my chair and buying me drinks that night. After the party, he showered me with attention; calling me, buying me flowers and begging me to go on more dates with him. I was reluctant, as my emotions from the breakup with Greg were still so raw, but he was so persistent and keen.

He kept telling me how good he could be for me and even the children, that he would never treat me the way Greg had done. He said he had saved some money and was happy to take care of me, just as he continued to care for his exes. I must admit that I liked what I was hearing, and I slowly fell for Aamon. I was still sure that I wanted and needed to move to Brisbane and if he wasn't trying to stop me doing that then perhaps, I could give another relationship a go. When I left for Brisbane with the children, we continued a long-distance relationship.

Over time we talked about our divorces, and I felt sorry for him when he described his marriage to his previous wife, Annette. He told me how he had done odd jobs, such as other people's ironing, to make extra money, so that they could get married and how much he missed her three children, whom he had become a father to and how he wished he still had contact with them.

He said that he had left her all the furniture and the house and paid all the school fees even after he had discovered she was having an affair with a local policeman.

Later I would discover it was all a big, fat lie. But right at that moment he still had me and I thought I had finally been sent the answer to my dreams. There were things which should have triggered alarm bells in my head.

I remember taking Courtney and Billy swimming with him at a local swimming hole and he stared intently at my daughter, who was eleven years old at the time. He made the point of asking me how old she was now, even though he knew and specifically pointed out that she was only five years off 16. A strange comment indeed.

He also used the word "sexy" a lot and in strange, inappropriate contexts – like "oh that's a sexy car" or "that's a sexy lounge".

He told stories of being a roadie for Kylie Minogue and commented on her sexual appetite, as if he had been a silent observer to these things. He also told stories of female hitchhikers he had picked up whilst driving his truck between Sydney and Cairns, but always told me how respectful he was to them. Making the point that he was not like other philandering long-haul truck drivers, with a girl in each town.

I was to find out over time that Aamon was a magnificent liar; the grandeur of his lies knew no bounds.

He had convinced everyone that he was a qualified builder. He would drive around Noosa with the kids and I in the car and point out all the houses that he had worked on, when he first arrived in Queensland. He wanted us to be impressed by his building prowess. The houses in Noosa were impressive homes and I remember thinking it was a lot of building work for one builder to do.

He told endless stories of designing a friend's Sydney mansion on a hilltop overlooking the Nepean river in Camden, outside of Sydney and described how their outdoor space and pool had been a concept in his mind that he had brought to fruition for them; of installing kitchens across the state of New South Wales and of running a profitable landscaping business in the rural town of Imbil just outside Gymthorpe.

When he was prompted for details of his builder's license, he said he couldn't remember his license number and the records for the tertiary education centre where he had done the written component of his training, had been destroyed in a fire. In the first instance, I just believed what he said; I had no reason to question his statement of facts, no cause for concern.

There were always elements of the truth in these stories he told, I would later discover. He did help with the Sydney home but only as the labourer, the pool and gardens were designed by a landscape architect. He did install kitchens but only in his local area in NSW and only as a labourer. The landscape business might have had business cards, but he had no business, no business receipts, no tax returns and he worked as a truck driver whilst running his supposed business. He never built any of the houses he showed us in Noosa; they were all built before his arrival in Queensland. It took me a very long time to find all this out.

Whilst in Brisbane we lived in the relatively new suburb of Forest Lakes. Courtney, my daughter, started high school and Billy, my son, was in primary school, where they both appeared to settle in easily and adjust to new life in a big city. However, I knew that the kids missed their Gymthorpe friends.

I had a wonderful job doing shifts at the Mater Children's Operating Theatre in South Brisbane. I was building a better life for us all, even if Aamon was still in Gymthorpe. I liked living on the outskirts of Brisbane. There were new and interesting friends, lots of places to go and see. A whole new world beckoned and I nearly broke free from the shackles of my old life. However, the tug of the devil and my inability to seek help for my still deepening anxiety and depression would bring an end to my break for freedom.

Aamon was desperate for us to return to Gymthorpe and move back into the house that I owned there. That house was the one thing that gave me a feeling of security. When everything else failed, I still owned that house. I loved it, had managed to keep it in the divorce settlement and had lived in it on and off since I had owned it. In the end I gave in. Long distance relationships were not easy, and I wanted to give Aamon and myself a chance, however much I enjoyed city life.

The kids were ecstatic to know they were going back home and relished the thought of getting back to school and their old routines, re-joining the local soccer club; playing netball and baseball; reconnecting with friends and their beloved grandparents. The kids had managed to have wonderful attachments and relationships with both my mother and my father. I realised how hard yet another move had been on them.

Just prior to the move back to Gymthorpe, Aamon and I were at a work function and he had received a phone call from my sister. I could see concern written on his face, but he refused to tell me what the phone call was about. I continued to enjoy the night but was troubled by Aamon's lack of enthusiasm for it. Eventually, I pestered the information out of him.

The children and my sister had been subjected to a home invasion and robbery at the house in Forest Lakes. The intruder had entered the house through the garage and had made it into my room, where he had proceeded to take my phone and search for money. At this point my sister had caught him and had chased him around the house trying to get him out of the home, fearful for the children. She had yelled for them to hide, but Billy had tried to stop the intruder and received a "clout" to the shoulder for his efforts. The puppy my sister had at the time had been kicked clear across the room and Courtney had tried unsuccessfully to grab the bag back from the intruder. My sister eventually cornered him and had him up against a wall in the kitchen, demanding he leave the house. She said it was obvious he was high and/or drunk and appeared disorientated and unable to leave the house. She released the intruder long enough for her to open the front door and for him to run out. They then called the police and Aamon.

I was so upset, so angry that Aamon had kept the information from me and not told me the instant he got the phone call. Once I knew what had happened, I demanded we go home immediately to check on everyone at home. It was the first time he intentionally kept vital information from me, but it would not be the last.

Moving back to Gymthorpe meant that I did not have a job to go back to, but there were some interesting prospects on the horizon. I was eventually offered a role as a project manager for a small rural hospital redevelopment in Kingaroy, another rural town about an hour and a half drive away from Gymthorpe. It was an opportunity to do something different, using my nursing skills and knowledge but without the rigors of clinical nursing.

It would mean long days with a lot of time away from the children and Aamon, and for this reason I nearly turned it down. Aamon encouraged me to "go for it"; pointing out that the money was great and the conditions of employment a dream. He assured me that he could cook, clean, iron and do washing so the kids would be well looked after. In the end I accepted the 12-month contract and started working full time. Travelling between Gymthorpe and Kingaroy proved exhausting, as I expected, but I enjoyed the work immensely.

I met some outstanding nurses and learned an incredible amount whilst doing the project. When the hospital redevelopment was completed, it was re-licensed and the operating theatres recommenced surgery after having been shut down for many years.

Driving backwards and forwards from Gymthorpe to Kingaroy gave me loads of time for reflection and even though I was happy with Aamon, I often thought of Andrew, curious to know what had become of his life. Many times, I drove past his parents' property, which was a detour from my usual route home, and wondered whether to say "Hi". But my doubts always got the better of me and I would drive on past. I thought he was probably happily married by then so what was the point?

During this time Aamon and I managed to save quite a bit of money. I decided to use the money to raise my house out of Gymthorpe's floodwater level. Aamon said he could do the work himself and I had no reason not to believe him. The development application required a builder to oversee the build, and Aamon said that he had to complete an extra course and do an exam to get an owner builder certificate. He said it was just a formality, on top of his original builder's license and I didn't question it. After the house was raised, and we added a big back deck, people began commenting on how the deck was laid upside down. Aamon said that his way was the right way and everyone else was wrong. How naïve I was; how easily I was manipulated and lied to.

This period was punctuated by numerous issues between my daughter, Courtney and myself. She was constantly arguing with Aamon about everything. It caused me endless sleepless nights of worry, but I put it down to teenage rebellion. After one huge argument, he removed the door from her bedroom, so she couldn't go into her room and lock herself in. He said she was not showing him the respect he deserved as her defacto stepfather, even though we were not married and if she didn't respect him, he wouldn't respect her either, in terms of her privacy. I made him put the door back on, but I begged Courtney to be nicer to him. It didn't work.

After another argument, he physically hit her according to Courtney. He denied it. I was caught between the man I loved and the daughter I loved, trying to choose who had the most to gain from lying about the situation. Eventually I told him that if he ever hit her again it would be his last act before he would be asked to leave.

I thought Courtney might need someone to talk to as she entered her teenage years. I finally found a psychologist and got her an appointment. Courtney went to about three sessions until Aamon convinced me that the sessions were a waste of time and money and he put a stop to them. He said we should know what she was talking to strangers about. As far as I was concerned it was a personal session between her and her psychologist, but it obviously worried him. At the time I just thought it was the difference in outlooks between a man and a woman but after talking to Courtney, I reluctantly agreed to let her opt out of them. After this time, though, she and Aamon seemed to fight less and talk more.

When she was 15 years old, Courtney attempted to take her own life by overdosing on Panadol. Luckily, she fitted and vomited up the drugs. I was, by this stage incredibly stressed both at work and at home. I tried desperately to help her, to talk to her, to assist her, but she kept pushing me away, seeming to turn to Aamon instead of me. The harder I tried the more she seemed to favour Aamon. I assumed it was because he was around more often than I was. I also remembered how stressful teenage mother-daughter relationships could be and felt grateful that Aamon was there for her to turn to.

There were times when I arrived home to find them deep in conversation which halted the moment they saw me. It hurt me as Courtney seemed to be punishing me, openly taunting me with her affection towards Aamon. I kept trying to gain rapport with her stubbornly not giving up.

As Courtney's behaviour deteriorated still further and to get some answers after her suicide attempt, I took her to the doctor for a mental health assessment and to investigate why she was not menstruating yet.

After the assessment the doctor asked to speak to me privately. He explained that it seemed Courtney was no longer a virgin.

I was shocked. She was still only fifteen and I naively thought that this was something we should have talked about openly, truly believing that we had enough of a relationship left, that we would have talked about something so important. Perhaps she had a boyfriend I did not know about; maybe this was the reason behind the suicide attempt, maybe this was why she was so moody.

When I asked Courtney about this, she insisted that she was not seeing anyone, much less sleeping with them. This information she volunteered without prompting, as the doctor had discussed this with her. It seemed that she wanted to talk to me about this, but I did not want to push her too much on it, worried that I would be breaching her privacy. I believed her, she had never lied to me before. I knew it was possible for this to happen during a sporting or horseback riding incident, but as Courtney did not ride horses, that option seemed unlikely. I was concerned but reasoned that her aggressive play on the netball court could have been responsible.

By this stage, I had other problems too. Aamon was drinking more and more, as well as driving over the limit, drink driving. I lost count of the number of times we argued about this. I offered to pick him up anytime, from anywhere, if he promised not to drink and drive, but he just did it anyway. The more I argued with him about it, the worse it got, to the point that I threatened to call the police on him if he ever did it again with either of the children in the car. He then explained to me that if he was arrested again, he would go to jail. He told me he had hit a police officer in the past when he was pulled over for a drink driving incident. He obviously had a problem I had not been aware of and I needed to help him. Knowing now what he did, I didn't think I had it in me to report him to the police, so our arguments continued.

He had many stories of 'bashing people' and there were also many boxing stories. He maintained he was a great boxer and had been extremely proficient in his early life. I found out in the end that none of it was true, but simply served to reinforce the illusion that he was big and powerful. He would play fighting games with the kids and he would pin them to the floor, making it look like fun, but after a while I realised it was a demonstration of his skill and might, reinforcing to the kids just how powerful he was.

He was not liked by everyone. I came across work associates who were so upset by a conversation with him that they refused to even speak to me. In hindsight I should have made them speak to me to find out what they were so upset about.

I discovered that there were also people who knew the depths of what I later discovered, like his ex-wife and his ex-girlfriend. There were those who suspected and said nothing me. I was too taken by him, so blinded by his lies and the illusion he created around us that I could not see any of it, could not uncover the truth.

When Courtney was in her last year of senior high school and Billy was in middle high school, Aamon managed to get a very well-paid job in Brisbane with a multinational construction company. This worldwide construction company had offices and work sites all over the world. Aamon had the use of a company car and a company phone. Aamon's new job was an enormous boost financially and made us more comfortable than we had been before. It also meant that Aamon was away during the week working in Brisbane and only came home on weekends. I was by now working within ten minutes of home at the local hospital and was home with the teenagers of an evening.

Courtney's behaviour continued to get worse towards me and the more I struggled to engage with her, the more she pushed me away. When he was home, Aamon made things worse by lavishing attention on Courtney, always buying her things and giving her affection and it often seemed this was at my expense, rather than an attempt to bring Courtney out of her black moods. He didn't do the same for me anymore, but I didn't say anything. I just worked hard to try and make a nice, happy family atmosphere. Even when I was just chatting with the two of them, they would often join forces and attack my opinion on something, saying I was inappropriate and unstable.

They would blame me for things that had happened in my own past and they could be vicious. Often it really was a case of them against me and I did not understand it for a minute.

By Courtney's seventeenth birthday she had her driver's license and no longer needed me to run her to and from school, or work or any of her social outings. I did worry that she did not seem to have much of a circle of friends or a boyfriend. She was not much of a socialite and seemed focused on her part time job, saving money and school.

I do remember now, finding Courtney and Aamon in bizarre situations from time to time. I just didn't think they were bizarre enough at the time to cause me to investigate further. Huddled together in the corner of the lounge whispering to each other, only to break apart when I entered the room and refuse to tell me about what they were discussing. I assumed that they were talking about me and all my faults. When I questioned Aamon, he told me not to worry and said that they were just teenage secrets that she did not want to talk to mum about. He said he was happy dealing with it and making my life less stressful. What did she think that she couldn't tell me, I wondered?

Sending them for groceries which would normally take half an hour, but would take them a couple of hours. Again, there was always a legitimate sounding response to my questions, like the queues at the checkouts were long or that they had stopped off for coffee at a coffee shop.

As I write this today, it sets off a deep physical reaction in me: nausea and sickness to the pit of my stomach. Aamon was, to all intents the father figure in the children's lives, and I knew it was nice that they wanted to spend time with him, especially Courtney. I knew how important a father figure was to a girl.

There were moments when I was definitely worried about the inappropriateness of Aamon's behaviour, trying to be unnaturally close to Courtney. I rapidly quashed those moments in my mind in the face of the reasonable excuses they both provided and refused to entertain such thoughts any further.

Retrospective remembering is difficult, but I remember the first instance of conscious fear about the relationship between Aamon and

Courtney. I was upstairs and calling Courtney to come up to tidy her room. After calling repeatedly I walked downstairs to find her curled up on the lounge with Aamon, watching television.

There was no evidence of any inappropriate behaviour, but they were very close on the couch. I tried to talk to Courtney by herself when she came upstairs, asking her if everything was alright with her and Aamon and if she was okay with him sitting so close to her, she just shrugged and said everything was fine. I think this was the first time I specifically asked her if inappropriate touching was happening, but she denied anything untoward was occurring.

Then Aamon came upstairs, I questioned him as to why he was alone downstairs with Courtney when there was a perfectly good television upstairs to watch. He said he thought I was watching a different channel upstairs and that they were watching TV downstairs. He hugged me and told me I worried too much about nothing, helped get the dinner on and cleaned up afterwards.

It was a horrible time, a lonely time and a time where there just did not seem to be any answers to the endless questions and searching in my mind.

There were a couple of more times that I asked Courtney about her closeness to Aamon. She kept denying that they were too close and Aamon kept telling me it was all in my mind and I was imagining things. In the face of periodical denial and lack of evidence, I did think that I was indeed going crazy. Intuitively I knew something was not quite right, but realistically there was no cold, hard evidence; only denial. It was Courtney's denial that Aamon was indeed too close to her that allayed my fears the most. I did not know then that she was trying to protect me from a truth that would simultaneously free her and imprison me.

For my daughter's work experience week towards the end of her senior year, Aamon insisted that Courtney do work experience with him at Loan Hire, in Brisbane. He thought she could do well in the construction industry. I was very much against the idea, wanting her to choose something closer to home; something more in keeping with her post-school desire of studying economics and journalism. But Aamon always got his way and allowing him to rail road her into work experience with him will be one of my biggest regrets in life. For it was during this time that he hurt her the most.

He went behind my back to organize her work experience placement with the school, producing a program of learning for her with his company which satisfied the school requirements. Courtney insisted she wanted to do it, saying she was excited at spending the week in Brisbane. They told me to "chill" and not make such a big deal out of it. I tried to arrange for Courtney to stay with my sister, just outside of Brisbane, rather than staying in the two bedroom flat with Aamon and his flat mate. Aamon overruled me.

I was deeply worried, but could not articulate the source of my worry into conscious thought enough to intervene in the situation. The reassurance from Courtney and the constant inference from Aamon that I was crazy and seeing things that weren't there, eroded my mind. I also began to think was I was verging on insanity. Every time I got to a breaking point, Aamon would pull out all stops and shower me with love and affection, gifts and praise, only to slowly erode it away until I got to the next breaking point and he would "reel" me back in.

I called Courtney several times during that week to check how she was going and see if she was enjoying her work experience time. She appeared cheerful and happy, talked about going to nice restaurants and visiting the big shopping centres in her time off. The last phone call before she came home did not go so well. Courtney cut me off and told me she was too busy to talk and that she would see me when she got home. Disappointed, I hung up the phone and looked forward to seeing her when she got home.

When Courtney came back from Brisbane, she was as cold as ice towards me. The more I plied her with questions about her time in Brisbane, the more she shut me out. I took her to lunch and afternoon tea, for mother-daughter time, but she was a closed book. Whenever I managed to get time alone with her at home, Aamon always miraculously appeared with an excuse of some sort and broke up our time together.

I found I was continually scheming to try and get time alone with my daughter.

Aamon changed as well after that work experience week and I had no idea why. Our relationship was so up and down that I accepted that we were just having another rough patch and it would pass in time.

Aamon also seemed to stop caring how he was behaving around me. I arrived home to find him viewing porn in the middle of the day. I thought it was my fault that he did this. I was willing, ready and able to indulge in the amorous side of our relationship, but he was increasingly not interested in me or our sex life. I'm writing this story retrospectively and even as I write, I'm questioning my own behaviour at that time. I did not know what was going on, I was concerned but had no concrete proof to act on. I was torn between Aamon and Courtney, reality and supposition. I was a mess.

I did think about leaving, or asking Aamon to leave, as the weight of suspicion that something was wrong seemed to be too much at times, especially after the work experience week. Every time I got close to making that decision, Aamon would lay on the charm, tell me he loved me, do something so thoughtful and loving that I believed all of the issues were in my imagination. It is all so clearly visible in retrospect, but so horribly dysfunctional at the time.

One of my greatest supports during that time was my boss at the Gymthorpe General Operating Suites. Her gentle massaging of my self-esteem kept me from completely succumbing to Aamon's taunts. I learnt as much about self-preservation and self-empowerment from this wonderful woman as I did clinical management. I'm sure she saw right through anything Aamon said, and I am sure she saw the devil in disguise, even when I failed to. Her friendship and understanding, not just as my boss, but as a friend was a blessing all through that time. It was her support and encouragement that helped me obtain a role in Corporate Queensland Health when we moved back to Brisbane.

More "not quite right" moments occurred. Aamon had an unusual friendship with a local council woman and her husband. We accepted many invitations to their place. After a few evenings with them Aamon told me he had had an affair with this woman long before we met, but he assured me that there was nothing between them now. I found it odd that she would invite someone she had had an affair with to socialise with her and her husband. I thought I might have been asked along for show. She was veracious, fun, open and very complimentary of Aamon, without appearing like there was anything between them anymore. They extolled the virtues of Aamon and what a great friend and confidante of the family he was.

Aamon did not seem interested in her anymore, but he seemed unnaturally interested in their youngest daughter. He was keen to take her for her first drink at the pub when she turned eighteen. I thought this was something which should be reserved for her family to do. I did not understand why her parents encouraged this behaviour from

Aamon. When I tried to say something, I was made to feel that I was somewhat of a "prude", that these were his long-time friends and that I should mind my own business.

I did, but it worried me nevertheless, as did other things he would suddenly disclose. After a party late one night he disclosed that he had seen his cousin sexually assaulted by an uncle. It was shocking at that moment and I was taken by surprise. He just blurted it out in a very drunken state, in front of my work colleagues. Trying to discuss it further in the light of day, saw him close the conversation and never mention it again. I discussed the disclosure with his sister at the time and she thought that it was about that time that Aamon's mother had tried to get him some counselling, but she was not sure what that was for. I wondered if this unsettling experience from his childhood was the spur for some of the inappropriate behaviour he displayed and his need to be important. Maybe this was why he was so inappropriate with people from time to time. This put to quiet, some of the concerns in my mind about Aamon. I saw a vulnerability that I had not seen before and I felt sorry that this had occurred in his life.

I found myself being kinder to Aamon and more tolerant of him and that led to a calmer situation at home. I focused more on Aamon and less on Courtney, who was still as hostile as ever.

Then Aamon proposed, not in a romantic way but at a family dinner in front of my parents. I was not sure how Courtney and Billy felt about this. Courtney remained very quiet for the rest of the dinner and Billy just smiled, gave me a hug and congratulated us. It was actually unexpected and I thought the timing was a little strange, but I was happy. It felt good to be engaged again and somehow legitimate in the eyes of the world.

We had a huge engagement party to celebrate the proposal. We tentatively set a date for the wedding in six months' time. Aamon did an amazing job of setting up the back yard with a huge marquee and lights throughout the back garden. He helped prepare the food and managed to socialise with everyone throughout the night. I was a lovely evening, with enough happiness and what I thought were genuine displays of love and affection from Aamon to settle the doubts that crept into my mind. Everyone seemed happy for us. Finally, I was getting my happy ever after.

Towards the end of that year, we made the decision to return to Brisbane so that Courtney could go to university to study economics and journalism and peruse a modelling career on the side to help fund her university studies. Courtney was tall, slim and gorgeous by this time. I had encouraged her interest in modelling and she had asked me to pay for various modelling and deportment courses which she diligently attended and excelled in. She had done some part time modelling for local boutiques and agencies on the Sunshine Coast.

The decision to move also meant that the wedding would have to be moved further back in the year to facilitate the expense of moving all of us to Brisbane. It would mean rewards for me career wise.

I wanted to try for a role at a corporate level in the Queensland Government's Health Department, for myself. I was still professionally ambitious and had often wondered what a role at this level of government would be like. Would I be able to effect change in health services at that level; would I have enough knowledge and ability to perform in a role at that level? I need not have worried as all my nurses training had prepared me perfectly to adapt and learn, particularly having worked in the fast-paced area of perioperative nursing. I got a great job coordinating the Maternal and Neonatal Network across the state.

It was meant to be a new beginning for all of us as a family, or that's how Aamon sold it to us all at the time. Retrospectively, I think it was an excuse to move us all away from friends and family who were fast starting to question the appropriateness of the closeness of Aamon's behaviour with Courtney. My family had never really taken to Aamon, even though he had provided for us and accepted the children into his life too.

Before we left Gymthorpe, Courtney was to attend her senior year school formal graduation and ball. Every mother anticipates helping her daughter plan a dress, order a car and organise the all-important hair and makeup appointments for the Senior Graduation. I was so excited for her and all her friends. We spent time shopping for her dress, planning her hair and makeup. For a brief, heady time, I felt like we were united again.

But Aamon interfered in all our plans. On the day of the event, having already paid a deposit and done a run through with the local hair dressers, Aamon suddenly announced he was taking Courtney down to the Sunshine Coast, an hour away, for her hair and makeup. I was so upset, so embarrassed to have to call and cancel the local appointments. I was so devastated that he had succeeded in ruining our special time together. We had planned to go to afternoon tea, then take Courtney to the appointment and then to come home and get her all dressed up. Now it was all ruined and it was all I could do to stop my own tears, so as not to ruin her night. She and one of her school friends were driven down to the Sunshine Coast by Aamon. I wasn't invited. When I protested, she gave me a look that stunned me into silence. Was this really what she wanted on that day or was she too being rail-roaded by Aamon?

They all arrived home at the last minute and getting her into her dress was a rush and not the relaxed photographic experience I had helped her plan. Aamon had reorganised the car she and I had planned, getting her something more expensive and better to take her to the formal. Such a lot of expense for a car that picked her up and dropped her off at the event.

He even supplied her with alcohol to take to the after party, when we had always had a strict rule regarding underage alcohol drinking. Aamon was openly encouraging her to drink and I know that was not something Courtney was keen to do. She had no experience with alcohol and had never shown or expressed an interest in drinking.

After the formal part of the evening, Courtney and her school friends were off to the after party together, with a designated driver. It should have been a time of joyful teenage fun and happiness for Courtney to remember, but it was forever tainted by Aamon's actions.

That night was also the first night Aamon acted rather strangely about Courtney staying out with her friends. He drove out to the graduation after party and insisted she accompany him home, even though it was well before her curfew. I didn't understand but I couldn't stop him, despite arguing with him to let her be and enjoy her time with her school friends. His counter argument was always that he was just being a protective father and how could I argue with him about that. He wasn't being protective; he was being domineering and not just over Courtney, but me and Billy too.

Not that he had much success with Billy. My son was the only one of us who ever truly stood up to Aamon and called him out on his behaviour.

Throughout my relationship with Aamon, Billy had maintained a close relationship with his own father, Daniel, and I encouraged him to spend time with his Dad; something that seemed to annoy Aamon. He tried a little to win Billy over by involving him in all his golfing endeavours. Billy loved golf and he was very talented and benefited from professional lessons up until we left for Brisbane. Back then Billy dreamed about turning professional one day, but he did not want Aamon to provide him with the route to the professional circuit. As a result, Billy never allowed himself to get close to Aamon. He loved me, and supported me, but tried to stay out of the family arguments when he could. He had a much larger circle of friends than Courtney did and this seemed to keep him very settled and stable throughout this whole time. Billy had always been an old soul, even as a young child, showing wisdom and understanding beyond his years.

I rarely argued with or had to discipline Billy when he was a teenager, he never caused me angst or worry. There have only been two times in his life that I have ever seen Billy out of control and angry. The first time was after Aamon had berated him for his loyalty to his father. I had stepped in and defended Billy and his right to have a loving relationship with his father, Daniel. I stated that this was not at the cost of a relationship with Aamon, but he could not let it go and just kept going on at Billy. Billy remained calm up until the point when Aamon overstepped the mark and said something completely derogatory about Daniel. I can't remember what the comment was, only that it caused Billy to stand up, fists clenched, face beetroot red and seething with anger, ready to defend his father. Aamon grabbed Billy with both hands by the shirt collar and looked like he was about to punch him, when I physically stepped in between them and threatened to call the police if Aamon laid a finger on Billy. Aamon skulked away with his tail between his legs. The only other moment was to occur soon.

After the move to Brisbane, Courtney looked to be in real anguish but insisted that she was doing just fine. At the time she was working very long hours at a local bistro and saving for another car. I kept trying to talk to her, but Aamon was always around when I tried to get time with her. Aamon promised Courtney that he could help her secure a big modelling contract worth at least a quarter of a million dollars, to be the face of a global company. It sounded good and I was hopeful that his negotiations on her behalf would pay off. He took us to meet the supposed bosses of the company, and we had lunch with them, met at their new premises and it looked legitimate. Aamon made me promise not to discuss Courtney's modelling contract over lunch, saying it was in the early stages of negotiation. This made sense to me, so I never actually talked to the company bosses about the contract. I would later discover that the whole modelling contract was a lie, used to keep Courtney quiet, so that she did not tell me what was happening to her. He used her dream to keep her silent

We rented a friend's tiny house in Victoria Point, on the coastal, eastern side of Brisbane. It enabled me to have a relatively short commute, by car or by train to my role in the suburb of Herston, Brisbane. I felt like a "fish out of water" in my new job. There was so much to learn and so many personalities to negotiate. It was a cut throat environment where staff did not think twice about standing on another's reputation or cutting people out to get ahead. For a country girl it was a rude awakening to truly dysfunctional corporate life. The role itself however, was wonderful; coordinating services, organising workshops. The most interesting and enjoyable part was the liaison with maternity clinicians across the state to implement changes to how maternity services were delivered.

Again, I was blessed with a manager who saw potential in me, who took the time to mentor and teach me. I loved the Maternal and Neonatal network but lacked the confidence to know that I was doing a good job. I felt that I would be better placed working in the surgical network or the anaesthetic network based on my clinical nursing experience working in operating theatres. I failed to realise that skills are transferable and no matter what your background, in corporate office it is about getting the job done and I was a master of that.

We finally set a date for the wedding, after much discussion: September, in the following year.

In January, Courtney celebrated her eighteenth birthday. She wanted a quiet little party and I started organising just that for her. A few old friends, a few new friends, lots of family; nibbles at a nice venue, flowers and a cake. Simple. Aamon barged in and reorganised everything. His idea was to celebrate her eighteenth at the dog races. My loud and vocal arguments were in vain, with Courtney quietly telling me to let it go and to cancel my venue. I cried for days, thinking that the dog races were no place for an 18-year-old girl to celebrate this milestone birthday. It wasn't the happy event it should have been, but Aamon always got his way. It was at this event that various members of the family made a point of commenting on how closely Aamon shadowed Courtney; how he was everywhere that she was he was, unless he briefly came to put his arm around me in a show of public affection.

On paper, writing about this today I look like a blind fool, but Aamon was a charming, manipulative liar who had me wrapped around his finger to the point that I did not feel able to decide things for myself. I thought that the issues with Courtney were because I was so flawed as a mother. It is only retrospectively that I know what he did and can see everything so clearly. I did not recognise what was happening as it was happening. For every argument between Aamon and I, there were apologies; we fell asleep in each other's arms at night; he never left the house without saying that he loved me.

Even with the little validation I received from family on that day, I still had no proof other than an uneasy feeling in the pit of my stomach. Aamon's gaslighting of me at any opportunity was working so well by now that I really did doubt my sanity and ability to see things clearly.

In understanding gaslighting I was able to understand why I was so stuck in this situation. It is a technique often used by narcissists, cult leaders, abusers and dictators where someone manipulates you by psychological means into doubting your own sanity. Aamon gaslighted me by telling me blatant lies and denying he ever said or did something, even though I knew he had. He used what was near and dear to me as ammunition; he wore me down over time; he used positive reinforcement to confuse me as he knew confusion weakened me. He aligned people against me; he told me I was crazy and that I was the liar. It is so clear to me now, but I had no knowledge of such behaviour back then.

Between the summer of January and the winter of July, life was completely hectic and chaotic. We moved three times in six months because the rental properties we were in either sold or did not want to renew their current leases. I organised a wedding, complete with venue, music, food and entertainment, together with a designer gown and beautifully made dresses for the bridesmaids. I got Billy into a new high school with new uniforms, new classes and subjects. I facilitated the sale of my home in Gymthorpe so that we could use that money to buy a block of land in Springfield Lakes where we were able to take advantage of a big discount on the purchase price of the land. Once the block of land was purchased, we went through the process of choosing a builder and started building a new house. All this whilst dealing with issues on and off at home.

I should have known it was all too much. The impact of the psychological warfare between Aamon and I, interspersed between the loving episodes, had me to the point where I battled suicidal thoughts. My emotions were like a roller coaster, feeling desperately out of control and still deeply worried about Courtney. She and Aamon still ganged up to berate me for so many things. Family and friends commented after this time that they were, by this stage, very, very worried about me on all levels.

Finally, totally overwhelmed by life in general, I sought help from a new doctor. Sitting in the doctor's office I could not stop my tears. He insisted that I stop work for the short-term, take some medication and see a psychiatrist. I was having my first mental breakdown; it was a long time coming and it would be a long, long trip to the other side.

I finally gave in and started the process of getting help. This change in working arrangements saw me at home alone for the first time in many, many years. It was both a blessing and a heartache, as I started the process of sorting out my internal dialogue and making sense of my life, my decisions and my pain.

Early in August that same year, the small hospital I had project managed had its official opening and I was invited to attend and unveil the plaque in commemoration of the day. It was an important milestone and would be attended by all the local dignitaries, council representatives and hospital hierarchy. I remember that morning specifically, as I had spent the morning talking to Courtney, which was so rare, and as I left to drive to Kingaroy, some one and a half hours away from our home in Springfield Lakes, Courtney gave me an uncustomary big hug goodbye. I left with a smile on my face.

Half way to Kingaroy, that day, I got another phone call from Courtney. She sounded very distraught and asked me to pull over off the side of the road and she had something to tell me. I pulled over, concerned that something was very wrong.

She asked if I could come home.

With the phone on loud speaker, I turned the car around to head home and I heard a door in the house closing, in the background of our phone conversation.

Courtney stopped talking and there was sudden change in her voice.

As I pleaded with her for more information about what she had to tell me, I could hear Aamon's voice in the background.

Courtney told me not to worry, that she just wanted to talk about moving out and that she would talk to me when I got home. I tried to reason with her, but she insisted that she was fine now, that she would just talk to Aamon. I explained that I was already on the way home, that I was there for her and I was happy to drive home to talk to her about moving out. My mind was also wondering why such a topic was causing her to be so distraught? She begged me not to come home and to go to the hospital opening that meant so much to me.

I wish I had gone home, wish I had listened to all my instincts and just gone home.

TONI LONTIS

Chapter

Day of Disclosure

"The conflict between the will to deny horrible events and the will to proclaim them aloud is the central dialectic of psychological trauma." JUDITH LEWIS HERMAN

Courtney never explained why the conversation about her moving out had caused her to be so distraught on the phone call she made to me whilst I was driving to Kingaroy. By the time I got home that evening she was back to her normal difficult self. The girl I had left that morning, the girl who had given me such a warm and loving hug, had retreated once again. I asked Aamon what she had discussed with him, but he just shrugged and said she just wanted to talk about moving out. I pressed him for the reason why this had upset her so much, but he just shrugged and said she was fine. For the next couple of days, on and off, I tried to break through the barrier Courtney had re-erected, but it seemed I had missed the moment.

About a week later, as I was preparing to go to lunch with a friend, Courtney rang to find out what I had planned for the day. When I explained I was going to lunch with Lisa, she asked if she could come too. I was so delighted to be able to have her come along with me and the thought of the day filled me with excitement. Courtney had taken to leaving the house very early in the morning, before anyone else was up and coming home when everyone had left for work and school. If I was home, we had been able to have some lovely chats about life in general and how things were going for her at work.

Courtney arrived home that day in time for a change of clothes before we set off to meet Lisa. As I was driving to our lunch date, Courtney offered to drive on the way home.

Despite being the end of August, the day was warm and clear, and the traffic flowed freely on the highway. Even the toll booths proved little hold up in an otherwise uneventful journey. Courtney seemed tired and I said she should consider cutting some of the long hours that she worked. She was focused on saving money for a deposit on a house of her own one day. She had a nice little nest egg building up and the overtime and weekend work certainly helped keep her bank balance healthy. I felt very proud of this hard-working young adult and chided myself for worrying about her so much.

We talked about Courtney's crush on one of the local boys. It had not gone down at all well with Aamon. He had made clear his opposition to her going on a date. I just brushed it off as Aamon trying to be an over-protective father.

I caught up on the latest gossip from Courtney's workplace and indulged in some all too rare laughs with her, as she talked about the differing personalities of her workmates at the local conference centre where she worked.

I was so happy Courtney was joining Lisa and I for lunch, it was a step in the right direction for our mother-daughter relationship and that excited me.

I was seeing things in a whole new perspective. I now felt that all the difficulties between Aamon and I were only small underlying problems in a normal relationship.

Only that morning he had held me in his arms, told me he loved me and that he could not wait to make me his wife.

It was going to be a beautiful Australian spring wedding. Everything had been planned perfectly. Orders had been placed; dresses made; decorations discussed and arranged; suits designed. There was going to be a gorgeous cake and great friends were coming. I saw it as a celebration to end all the ups and downs of the five-year relationship to date: a new way forward, whatever our future held, I felt sure that we could face it together.

I was so excited to be spending time with my favourite people and the conversation flowed easily, all focused on the upcoming marriage, in two weeks.

My best friend was a little older and wiser than me and I valued her experience and counsel when I needed it most. I had met Lisa years earlier at the small private hospital in Gymthorpe, where we both worked, and we had become friends. She had moved to the Glitter Coast from Gymthorpe about eighteen months before we moved to Brisbane and we had gotten closer since that time. In Lisa there was a loving friendship that was unconditional.

As I got older and understood more about life, I recognised the many elements that had shaped the decisions I had made and knew some of those decisions were not always for the best. Lisa just wanted to make sure this marriage was a good decision. I had no idea the direction that would take.

As I pulled the car into the car park, I felt a bizarre shiver of foreboding. "Come on girl" I whispered under my breath. "Shake off the doldrums. You are going to enjoy today."

Lisa looked immaculate, as usual; her blond hair freshly coiffured into a bob, her makeup applied perfectly and wearing a comfortable linen dress that made her look every bit like the 'Glitter Coaster' she was.

Our conversation quickly moved through the pleasantries and on to the wedding plans, and in true girly fashion we pored over all the fine detail of the day. While I chatted on excitedly, I noticed Courtney was very quiet, appearing to lose interest in the wedding conversation. She was toying with her food, moving it from one side of the plate to the other.

Lisa and I both were both stealing glances at Courtney. I was just about to say something, but Lisa spoke first.

"Courtney," said Lisa. My daughter looked up and for a second, I saw a flash of that anguish which I had seen in her face before, but then it was gone. I watched as she seemed to visibly compose herself "I think it's time you told your mother," Lisa said gently, "Has he been abusing you, Courtney?"

My mouth dropped opened. What? I looked at my friend and then at my daughter. What did Lisa mean? Who?

That sense of foreboding I had felt in the car park came rushing back and as I waited for my daughter to laugh and deny Lisa's question, I watched the colour drain from her face.

Her pallor changed from pink to blue grey as she slowly nodded her head.

I felt my heart stop in my chest. I was finding it hard to form words, breathless like I had been punched in the stomach.

Finally, all I could blurt out "Is this true, are you sure?' to which Courtney responded, in a voice not much above a whisper, "Yes, Mum."

In those few seconds my whole world seemed to stop moving; everything appeared to go into slow motion; all background sounds died down and people disappeared from my peripheral vision. The world around me just stood still. It became a slow, deathly quiet place, even though we were in a restaurant in the middle of a busy shopping centre.

I cannot remember much of what happened in those moments after my daughter's disclosure; the stunned silence seemed to last for hours.

It was only broken by Lisa's next words, "I don't need to know what happened, but your Mum does." She reached across and touched Courtney's hand in encouragement, as if she understood what Courtney was going through.

I looked at Lisa. How did she know to ask that question? Did she have a hunch? Why here, why now?

I don't remember feeling the slightest bit of animosity towards Lisa, just confusion as to how she could know to ask this of my daughter. I would discover years later that Lisa knew from her own experience the signs of an abused teenager; had recently recognised in Courtney her need to escape from the tortuous hell of the abuse Aamon was subjecting her to.

Right there, right then, my life changed forever. Our lives changed forever.

What had been happening under my roof, in my home and right in front of me was being confirmed by the person who had denied it for so long. It was like the fragment of a horrid dream coming into full focus, from which there was no awakening.

I felt nauseous, unsteady and in real pain, right in the centre of my chest like a blowtorch was being thrust at my heart.

Tears welled in Courtney's gorgeous eyes, now only to pour down her face, her pupils dilated, hands wringing in despair. Her body and shoulders drooped in resignation of the inevitable knowing and the sad little nodding of her head in confirmation.

I knew, beyond a shadow of a doubt that this was the truth. This information simultaneously filled in a picture and confirmed the very darkest fear that had been hidden in the depths of my heart; a fear that required absolute proof before action; a fear that I finally had to face;

a fear that once confirmed would set my daughter free.

I felt like I had just been handed the final piece of a giant jigsaw puzzle that that I had been trying to put together for years; but instead of a wondrous finished landscape, it revealed a darkly distorted picture of secrets, lies, pain and suffering. I had tried to put this puzzle together so many times before, tried to make sense of it, but I had never been able to get the pieces to fit where they should, until now.

It was without a doubt the single most horrifying moment of my entire life.

It would take some time for me to understand the immense courage my daughter had displayed on that day of disclosure. Many in her situation would not have had the strength, willingness or courage to do so. So many victims hide their terrible secret until they are much older; some take their secrets to the grave.

Of all the things I had done wrong up until that point, I know, that on that day and in that moment, I did everything right.

I reached across the table for Courtney's hand, tears welling in my eyes, as I searched her face for some indication that this was all a big mistake. There was no denial evident in Courtney's eyes. I told her it would be okay and that whatever had happened we would face it together.

The truth was now known by the three of us at that table and it would not be long before many others would find out. I wasn't aware of the depth of depravity that had befallen my precious girl. In my naivety, I had no idea of the extent of what Aamon had done. I did not let my mind consider the possibilities.

I could see that Lisa was struggling with the enormity of the moment too. I understood her urgent need to rush from the restaurant. I did not understand that in the moment of disclosure, Lisa would be compelled to deal with reliving her own painful past. It was too much for her and Lisa excused herself from lunch.

My daughter and I were left, sitting in a roomful of strangers, trapped in our own private worlds, both wondering where everything went from there.

Chapter

The Aftermath

> *"In order to escape accountability for his crimes, the perpetrator does everything in his power to promote forgetting. If secrecy fails, the perpetrator attacks the credibility of his victim. If he cannot silence her absolutely, he tries to make sure no one listens."*
> JUDITH LEWIS HERMAN

Courtney had her head bowed like she was waiting for a verbal or physical onslaught; she wouldn't meet my eye. She looked about five, waiting for punishment after she and her brother had broken a vase or been fighting with each other. Back then that would have seemed important. Now nothing seemed important except my broken child, sitting in front of me, having been subjected to so much hurt, humiliation and horror by someone I brought into her life. I had no idea what to say. Instead I reached out and put a hand on her shoulder. Instantly I felt her deflate, like someone had let all the air out of a balloon, and her full body weight came to rest against my hand. Then she was in my arms and holding me like we were in the teeth of a hurricane. A surge of love pulsed through me. I couldn't remember the last time she had held onto me, had truly needed me, and just feeling her body against mine opened the floodgate to my tears. This was my child and more than ever now I had to fight for her, help her, heal her. Nothing else mattered but giving her back everything, he had taken away; everything I had taken away.

"Shall we get out of here," I whispered, and she nodded.

I have no idea how we walked out of that restaurant, calmly and coolly, as if nothing had happened, as if my whole life as I knew it, hadn't ended right there on that blue and green lino floor. I had no idea where it was going but I finally knew Courtney and I were going together. I felt like my whole body was held together with sticky tape and glue, about to fall apart at any minute.

Courtney walked like a tin soldier at my side. She took the keys from me and insisted she drive home. I protested, but then realised my hands were physically shaking, as much as my body was. Courtney guided me gently into the car. It didn't make sense. I should have been looking after her, but she was caring for me.

"You're in shock Mum," she said kindly. How long had it been since she had spoken so kindly to me? I felt like I had been flattened by a bulldozer. As she drove the car out of the car park all I could see was Aamon and my daughter together; Aamon leaning over her; dom-inating her, scaring her. What had he done to her? Abused? What did abused mean? Kissing? Touching? Worse? When had it started? When she was younger or just recently? How? When? Had I been in the house? Sleeping?

"What did he do?" I heard myself blurt out, and immediately wished I hadn't, but I had to know.

If he had just touched her, maybe we could navigate our way through that. She and I. Not Aamon and I. But by the agonised look on Courtney's face, I immediately knew it was a lot more than that.

Courtney began to talk, almost like an automaton as she drove, and with each sentence that she spoke I felt my whole body go more and more numb.

The more she talked the lighter her being seemed to appear, truly like the disclosure of her pain had lightened her body.

"He sexually assaulted me, over and over again," she said. I put my hand on her shoulder again. "It's okay. That's enough for now," I said. "It's over."

In a sudden moment of clarity, I knew what to do and was spurred into action.

Firstly, as Courtney drove us home, I called the police and reported what I knew.

Courtney had begged me not to do this. It was obvious that she did not want to get Aamon into any trouble. I felt a surge of pure rage and anger, not with Courtney but with Aamon.

"Like hell we are not reporting this to the police" I muttered under my breathe, hoping she would have time to get her head around it by the time they talked to her. I was not prepared for this to be swept under the carpet by anyone and I was furious that even now, Aamon seemed to be calling the shots in her mind. In my state, at the time, I called 000 and was put through to the appropriate police station. I remember vaguely talking to a police officer who took down our details and a sketchy description of the crime. He then made a time to come to our home to question Courtney, later that night. She was still protesting as I hung up the phone. I was very firm with her and stated that she had to at least talk to the police officers and then we could decide what the next steps would be.

Secondly, I sent Aamon a text message saying, "Don't come home, I know everything, the wedding is cancelled, and I never want to speak to you again."

I was shaking with so much rage and fury that I had to retype the text message numerous times to get it right. I did not trust myself to ring and talk to him in person. I wanted to kill him; inflict the pain on him that I was feeling. How could he think that he was ever going to get away with this? I wanted to dismember parts of his anatomy, so that he could never hurt another person again.

I was also simultaneously concerned that he would want to talk to Courtney before she spoke to the police, to try to talk her out of reporting his crimes, to frighten her into silence. My heart was beating so fast I thought it would jump out of my chest.

His response was as I expected, "what's going on, what has Courtney said?" Confirming in my mind that he indeed knew exactly what was going on and what was being said. I did not care where he went that night and, in the days, ahead; did not care that he had no clothes for work the next day; did not care how he survived. In that moment I hated everything about him. I knew I had to keep Courtney safely away from him and this was the only way I knew how.

My hands are again shaking as I type this passage, some 11 years later.

Thirdly I rang my parents. I told them that Courtney had just disclosed that she had been sexually assaulted by Aamon and that I needed them to come down and stay with us. I thought that with my father staying at our house, Aamon would not dare to try and come home.

Once again, I was feeling ashamed that I needed them; dismayed to be dragging them into such a sordid situation, but I realised then how much I needed to have them there.

Lisa rang to say that she and her husband would be arriving later to support us whilst the police did their interview, in case my parents didn't arrive in time. I hated my neediness at that moment, but I also knew that the kids needed kind and gentle support around us at that time.

When I hung up from my parents, I looked across at Courtney and saw the strangest emotion in her eyes. Hope. Hope that perhaps the storm clouds had lifted. Hope that things could be different. Hope for a better future. For one moment my anguish lifted too, as I looked at the sudden new light in her. It would not last for long and it would be a long time before I saw it again.

We arrived home and went into the house. Suddenly the bedroom I loved appeared tainted with shame, the lounge room shrouded in sadness, my dream kitchen coated in lies, the white leather couch in the family room muddied with pain and suffering. Where had my sanctuary disappeared to? I knew the house I once loved was now sullied with my daughters' suffering. I hugged Courtney again before she disappeared to take a long shower and I sat down with a cup of tea and my thoughts. Mostly I remember the terrible darkness that descended on the home and the thoughts of how I was going to explain everything to Billy.

When Billy did arrive home from school, I sat him down in the lounge room and explained that Courtney had been hurt by Aamon. There was no way I was going to be able to hide this from him. For only the second time in his life I saw a blind anger and rage line my 16-year-old son's face. I could feel the tension rise in his body and he asked if Aamon was coming home. When I explained that I had asked him to stay away, Billy's response was, "If he ever comes near you or Courtney again, I will kill him."

In that moment I was simultaneously proud of my son and terrified for what he would do if he ever saw Aamon again. I had a terrifying thought that maybe Billy had been hurt by Aamon too.

"Has he ever touched you, Billy" I asked, looking deeply into my son's eyes.

"No", Billy said, "He wouldn't because Dad would kill him if he did."

I then wanted to know if he had ever seen or witnessed Aamon hurting Courtney and this he denied any knowledge of as well.

Billy's initial rage was now replaced by a look of deep sadness and worry for his sister, as if he was understanding for the first time why things had been so messed up between us all. We talked about the fact that the family was arriving to stay for a little while and that the police had to come to talk to Courtney. After this he disappeared to his bedroom to await the events of that evening.

My overwhelming feeling during those hours in the lead up to everyone arriving, was one of guilt and remorse in equal measures combined with nauseousness and the ever-present pain in my chest. I did not quite know what to do, but that was soon replaced by a stream of calls and text messages from Aamon.

He just kept calling and messaging both Courtney and me.

On one phone call to me, he called Courtney a liar and that it was all a complete fabrication. In another call he wanted to know how old she was saying she was at the time of the alleged assaults and kept asking if she was saying she was under 16 years of age!

The police arrived several hours later, two men, very professional and matter of fact. They showed no empathy for anything Courtney was going through, anything she was saying. They wanted to interrogate Courtney immediately and they did not want me to listen to their questioning. This was a little hard, as the interview was conducted in an open area in the small lounge between Courtney and Billy's bedrooms.

Everyone in the house could hear snippets of what was going on.

I wish I had insisted they go into a room, or that they had let me sit with her during that time.

I could hear Courtney protesting to their line of questioning and refusing to answer in the depth of detail they wanted. Courtney was being asked about being raped, where, when and the specific circumstances. She was crying, sobbing and begging them to stop making her tell them her story.

Courtney was an 18-year-old girl having to explain to two male detectives the depravity she had suffered. So horrid was the initial interrogation that I was physically sick, and I ran into the room and begged them to stop. I was sick to the pit of my stomach at the fragments of information I could hear. I was sick because Courtney appeared to be suffering so much and I wanted her suffering to stop.

Retrospectively, I knew that the police would be asking detailed questions of Courtney and wanting to know exactly what happened but, in my naivety, and shock, back then, it was harrowing. I was unprepared for the length of time it took for Courtney to discuss the depth and extent of Aamon's alleged offending, even if I did not know the exact details.

The detectives explained that they had to be sure of her allegations before handing over the case to the Child Protection Unit. There was a brief discussion regarding potential charges, the police stated that the Child Protection Unit and the district prosecution team would determine exact charges after further interviews and investigations. Even though Courtney was 18 years old at the time she had disclosed, most of the crimes had been committed before she was 18 years old and her memory at that first interview only detailed crimes after she was 16 years of age. The detectives felt sure that she was telling the truth and that it warranted further investigation by the Child Protection Unit.

I asked if they had sent someone to arrest Aamon. The police officers said that at that stage they were unable to arrest anyone. Their role was only to hear the allegations from Courtney, assess the truthfulness of the allegations and then refer the case to the Child Protection Unit for investigation, formal gathering of statements and perhaps subsequent arrest. I was astounded to hear this, but too exhausted to give it further thought.

As much as I wanted Aamon arrested that night, they said they couldn't do it and there was nothing I could do about it in that moment. Apparently, arrests don't happen as easily as they do on the television. That night was the first time I started to question our judicial system here in Australia. The thought of Courtney having to tell her story repeatedly made me really angry.

Courtney was by now utterly exhausted and snuck away to the solitude and darkness of her bedroom.

As the police left, they gave us detailed information as to where we had to be the next day so that Courtney could give her formal statements.

Then the family and friends gathered for a coffee around the dining room table and the rest of the evening was a mishmash of people, conversations, tears, anger, dismay and pain. No one talked about the actual allegations very much. The focus was more on how to protect Courtney and how to stop the constant barrage of phone calls and messages we were all getting from Aamon. To try to protect Courtney, I wanted to keep the "circle of knowledge" around what had happened as tight as possible.

I also needed to let everyone know there would no longer be a wedding.

By the time all the friends left, and I had settled my parents into a room for the night, it was late. When I finally crawled into bed, as tired as I was, I could not stop my mind racing.

As I tried to go to sleep Courtney arrived beside my bed and asked if she could sleep beside me, saying she felt safer in my room, than her own. I threw back the covers and in she jumped, like the small child she had once been.

We lay there, side by side in silence for a few moments and then she suddenly began to talk.

Courtney seemed to be recalling whatever came to her mind first, not always in a consecutive order.

She told me she was going to tell me the day I had driven to Kingaroy. She had finally gotten up enough courage to do so and had picked a time when she felt sure Aamon would not be home or likely to come home.

I was shaking just hearing her speak.

Her confession was thwarted by Aamon, who arrived home unexpectedly. I heard the change in her voice that day. He silenced her with an assault on our bed. I tried to choke back my tears, desperately not wanting to upset Courtney anymore, desperately hoping that her disclosure would help her healing. I didn't want to know these things and I hate writing about them today.

I held her close that night, never wanting to let her out of my sight again, my woman child, my daughter, my hero.

These conversations would occur each night and go on into the early hours of the morning, as she unravelled the nightmare her life had been and what she had endured. For the next 6 weeks or so this was our nightly pattern, I would go to bed and Courtney would come and jump in beside me. I would listen in the darkness, holding her hand with tears bucketing down the sides of my face, desperately trying to keep my tears from her and hoping that somehow, I was helping. It did seem to bring solace to her. What could I do but listen to the depravity of what she'd been through? The more she talked the more doubt was removed from my mind, there was too much, too often, too depraved, too horrible, not to be true. It left me with a physical pain in my soul, a blinding anger that would take years to subside and a desperate need to heal my daughter from her pain.

I never felt anything but compassion for my child. I would not allow myself to apportion any blame to her at all. Despite my mind being filled with hideous images of Aamon's crimes, I refused to let my mind go to that place and constantly pushed the images from my mind.

Over those nights she recalled a time when she was being molested and I had walked into the room. All I saw was Courtney lying in bed and looking very tired and distressed, with Aamon sitting on the bed talking to her. I immediately berated Aamon for keeping her awake when she obviously needed sleep and banished him from the room. That night he would not go, but I stubbornly insisted Courtney needed sleep and stayed in the bedroom doorway until he left. Courtney said that he had been molesting her that night and that she was thankful I had stepped in when I did. My poor darling girl, I had managed to protect her once without even knowing it. I was sickened by his blatant evil.

Another night she recalled the argument Aamon had had with Billy about his father. I remembered that day too. I had stopped the argument and after everything had settled, I had gone to get groceries for school lunches the next week. Whilst I was out and Billy was in his bedroom with the music turned up loud, he assaulted her again.

She further disclosed the worst of assaults happening when she joined Aamon's firm for work experience in Brisbane. She was subjected to days of molestation and assaults, two hours away from her mother and brother. Courtney described the duality of fear she felt at that time, fear of telling me and fear that Aamon would hurt me or Billy if she told anyone. Fear kept her silent.

I now understood her coldness when she returned home. What my poor girl had to endure was horrendous.

The wedding of my sister at a beautiful mountaintop retreat in Maleny on the Sunshine Coast, in Queensland was another time Courtney spoke of during our sessions. The whole family had gathered to celebrate, and we were all staying at the resort. Whilst everyone else was up dancing and having fun, Aamon made Courtney go the room we were sharing, not the room she was sharing with Billy. He hurt her again that night and when she didn't return and I questioned Aamon, he told me that she had gone to bed early because she had a headache. I wish I had checked on her that night but instead I asked her the next morning how her headache was? This just spurred a volatile reply that stopped me asking further questions.

She spoke of the many times he would drop home during working hours, when he knew she was at home and Billy and I were absent. Always when there was no one around to protect her from his onslaughts.

Courtney said he used to touch her right in front of people, in public places, behind my back, knowing that she would not make a fuss, confident in not getting caught, assuming he had silenced her for good. She was so scared to tell, fearful of what Aamon would do to Billy, to me, to her grandparents.

Every morning after a night time disclosure, I woke up with the true enormity of what had happened hitting me like a battering ram.

The wedding and all the arrangements which I had so carefully put into place, had to be cancelled. My mother and Lisa were there, thankfully, to help me sift through everything.

I have been asked if I ever felt any animosity towards Lisa, but of course I haven't. I have only ever felt an enormous debt of gratitude to her. Had she not had the insight to ask Courtney that question that day, I may have actually married this man and his attacks on Courtney would have continued on and on. Lisa showed great strength of character that day in doing what she did, risking my reaction and Courtney's denial.

Somehow, between us, we managed to let everyone know without giving too much information, that the wedding was off. The girls, my mother and Lisa, rang those that had to travel the furthest and to the others they wrote a little note to post, saying something along the lines of "Unfortunately the wedding has been cancelled due to unforeseen circumstances. This is a deeply distressing time for Toni and her immediate family and we ask that you respect her request for privacy at this time. Toni may contact you at some stage in the future to explain what has happened, however until that time we ask that you do not try to contact her."

Most people did not question any further, but Aamon's family did not let up. Over the course of the next few weeks I had to endure phone calls from many of them seeking answers. They did not accept what Courtney was saying. She and I were subjected to name calling and abuse. The truth is so hard to swallow for some people. It shattered Courtney to know that they did not believe her.

These were people that I loved and trusted, and their disbelief of Court-ney was almost too much to bear. They knew me, they knew my kids, they must have known that Courtney wasn't lying, but they stuck by Aamon. I will never understand it because he not only lied to us, but he lied to and deceived them too.

There was so much grief that I was numb for months. In my already weakened mental state, I'm really not sure how I got through those months, not sure how I made sense of anything. I did know that talking to a counsellor helped and that the medication finally worked but the darkness of depression still beckoned.

I was not comfortable taking antidepressants, but the doctor was insistent I needed something to help me cope. The medication helped my brain with the trauma it was experiencing at that time. It lifted my mood and eased the tears that seemed to be an hourly occurrence. I reluctantly agreed that I really was broken and would do just about anything to alleviate my sadness.

The first counsellor I spoke to was a jolly Irish woman who encircled me with love and understanding. She was recommended to me by my doctor and in my initial stages of grief, suffering and anger, she was really helpful. She was truly appalled at hearing my story and set about giving me small tasks to assist in dealing with the anger and sadness I felt. She gave me a deeper understanding of what the victims of these crimes go through and was the first to express what an amazing job I did in the first hours after Courtney's disclosure. I did not know that some mothers, upon hearing their child's disclosure, refuse to act, refuse to believe their child, refuse to call the police. That was beyond my comprehension.

The endless explanations were the worst because not everyone was understanding or empathetic. From having to talk to Billy's school, answer the neighbours wondering where Aamon had disappeared to and to the banks to try to sort out the financial affairs, it was all torture. I remember a particularly terse and non-sympathetic conversation with my own brother, questioning how I had let this happen to his niece.

It was difficult to gauge people's intentions, too. There was one particular person who, retrospectively I found out, was faking her concern and asking way too many pointed questions, just to see what Courtney was telling the police and then reporting directly back to Aamon. I hope that one day she is able to reflect on her behaviour and see just how wrong she was. How duplicitous of someone to do that?

The process of giving police statements, the week after disclosure, was an arduous one. Courtney spent two eight-hour sessions with police. This was followed by my statement and my parents and friends' statements, over the course of about two weeks.

Billy was also summoned for a statement. We were not allowed to know what was in anyone else's statement at the time it was made, it was only subsequently that I learned what was said. Billy's statement was sealed and protected due to the fact he was a minor. He was also appointed a court support officer to go with him during the taking of his statement and also during his closed court appearance. I was not allowed to be with him, as I was considered a witness too and you are not allowed to corroborate (have knowledge of) other witness statements.

Once the statements were collated, prosecutors then had to decide what to charge Aamon with. At this time, Aamon was still free to walk the streets, which was ludicrous in my mind!

The police wanted to charge Aamon with carnal knowledge, because even though he was not Courtney's father or her step-father, he was my defacto partner. Under Australian law, de facto relationships are treated as marriages. Aamon was my partner and therefore considered stepparent to my children.

Courtney's case would become a test case which would later be used to educate new defence lawyers; a case to test the new Defacto/step-parent incest laws, in Queensland. I wish Aamon had simply been charged with sexual assault and Courtney's case had not been used as a test case. The fact that is was a test case backfired on us later.

There were supervised phone calls, called pretext phone calls, to try to get Aamon to admit on tape to what he had done. Courtney had to go to the Child Protection Unit and set up a phone call between herself and Aamon. This was incredibly stressful for her, but she did it and did as the police asked. Aamon was too cunning; and he knew and indicated he knew he was being taped.

Surprisingly Aamon was only ever interviewed twice by the police and let go pending further investigation. It was terrifying for Courtney who knew she might run into him anywhere.

It took about nine months before Aamon was finally arrested and formally charged with eight counts of carnal knowledge of an offspring. For me this wasn't enough. Of the hundreds of assaults and molestations that took place, it came down to eight counts!

What I did not know then, is that to charge a person on an indictable offence, each offence must be placed to a time and a location of the crime. If the victim is unable to provide this information the police are unable to charge the perpetrator with a crime. This is not a discussion that is had with the victim, you are at the mercy of the District Prosecutor and what he sees as a likely legal outcome of getting a guilty verdict. The charges of carnal knowledge were based on new Queensland laws which allowed charges against step-parent fathers or defacto fathers for offences perpetrated against children in their care. Courtney was considered in Aamon's care.

Despite the gravity of his crimes, Aamon was charged and immediately released on bail, pending a trial date.

Even in those early stages, Courtney seemed to have a whole chunk of memory loss between the ages of eleven years old and fifteen years old. Her memories start to fade after the age of eleven with hardly any memory at all of things that happened in her life from the age of twelve and then they fade back in at the age of fifteen. We will never know if the abuse happened during those years as her memories cannot be reached, a retrograde amnesia protected her innocent mind.

This fits the picture of Post-Traumatic Stress Disorder (PTSD). Freudian psychology suggests that amnesia is an act of self-preservation, where overwhelming anxiety or even suicide may result from acknowledgment of the traumatic event. Unpleasant, unwanted or psychologically dangerous memories are repressed or blocked from entering the consciousness mind. This process acts as a kind of subconscious self-censorship. The memories remain stuck in the unconscious mind. Neurologically, normal memory processing is blocked by an imbalance of stress hormones such as glucocorticoids and mineralocorticoids in the brain, particularly in the regions of the limbic system involved in memory processing.

Courtney, Billy and I were harassed endlessly by Aamon in the lead-up to the trial. We were followed in our cars and watched from the street. We received thousands of phone calls and hundreds of text messages until we blocked his number, only to have him call on a different number until we blocked those calls as well. These messages mostly revolved around his professed love for me. "How could I believe Courtney's lies," he demanded. "Can't we just forget this and get married.". "How was he supposed to keep working with all this going on?", he wanted to know, as if trying to arouse some pity for himself. When this failed, he proceeded to berate me about how much money I owed him for the deposits on the wedding events.

He asked how he could hold his head up in public anymore. Short, constant and distressing, trying to evoke responses from me.

To Courtney he wrote about how much he missed her; how much he loved her, how he could work it out so that the police were not involved. He asked her how she could tell me and told her that I was eventually going to blame her and hate her.

He tried to isolate Courtney in car parks and dead-end roads. He chased her and pursued her endlessly. The police did not seem to take it all that seriously and failed to intervene on our behalf. Apparently, they would have acted if he had physically hurt any of us. It was a farce. A dangerous, upsetting farce.

We received letters written by him, pretending to be someone else, telling us that Courtney was lying. People I considered to be my friends as well as his friends called to plead his innocence, on his behalf.

Aamon even called 000 (emergency services) claiming that he was sheltering behind the water tank in the back yard of our home in Springfield Lakes, Queensland, because we had a gun and were trying to kill him. He was calling from Sydney. We were raided by the police in full tactical uniform at three o'clock in the morning. It was terrifying as they burst in the front door with their guns drawn and shouted orders at us to get down on the ground, demanding to know where the gun was. Luckily for us the team quickly realised we had no gun, we were all in bed, and Aamon wasn't hiding out the back. We made them tea, apologised and had them laughing by the time they left, although we were very shaken by the incident.

Then we were all summoned to the police station to listen to the 000-emergency call and verify that it was his voice. There was no doubt, it was. We all made statements confirming this. We were promised he would be charged for this crime as well, but he never was!

After the hoax emergency call, we were finally able to apply for an apprehended violence order (AVO) to prevent him from coming within 100 metres of us and ensuring he would go to jail if he contacted us in any way. Even with this in place he still tried, until I called the detective on our case in tears asking for her to intervene. Apparently a quiet "off the record" talk was had with him and the harassment finally ceased.

Then he started writing to other people instead of us. He wrote to the hospital where I had worked and lodged a breach of privacy complaint against my old boss. What he hoped to achieve is uncertain, however the angst he caused my old boss was disgraceful. She had to plead her case to the Director of Nursing and explain the whole background of the story, which was mortifying for me.

Aamon also lodged a formal complaint against the police officer who had accompanied him to our home, when he had demanded the return of more of his "things". The lovely young constable had done absolutely nothing wrong and was just in attendance to keep the peace and ensure we were in no danger. Aamon stated that the police officer had made derogatory remarks to him, and then escalated the complaint to the next level in the police department. I received a call from the District Superintendent to assist with their enquires, because I had been at the house with Aamon and the police officer the whole time. I was a witness to the fact that the police officer had not made any comments other than pleasantries and the introduction of himself and why he was there. I will never understand the stupidity of such actions, as they only cemented in everyone's mind the delusions of this man.

After the initial text message I sent, telling Aamon not to come home, he moved in with a male work colleague and friend who lived in Brisbane. This friend had two teenage daughters. Such was the dismay of the two girls to have an "alleged rapist" (this is the word the girls used in their phone call) in their midst they called a local radio station, to ask for help and highlight their plight. The two girls were referred to the Child Protection team for assistance. The girls said he was watching them undressing and trying to see them shower. Lord knows what their father was thinking, but I can only assume he thought Aamon was innocent.

During this time, I also needed to sort out our finances. I had been left with all the joint liabilities, and I was also trying to make the mortgage payments on our new home while I was not working. Aamon refused to pay any of his share of the mortgage, the car loan or the credit card. The only way I could make him do this was to pursue a financial settlement.

I had to pursue a financial separation outside of the criminal court case. I had been advised that it would have been better to wait until the criminal court case was done before seeking a financial settlement. The court would have viewed the financial settlement in my favour, had the criminal case been finalised with a guilty verdict. However, by now I was so close to bankruptcy that I needed to do the financial settlement sooner rather than later. The compounding worry of two separate court processes, criminal court and family law court, was debilitating. Finally, the Family Law court mediation arrived much sooner than the Criminal Court case.

Aamon had a horridly arrogant solicitor for the family court mediation for financial separation, who made the whole process a misery. To top it all off, I ended up having to pay Aamon fifty thousand AU$!! He came to the relationship with a beat-up old car, mismatched run-down furniture and few savings. He left with my daughter's virginity, my soul and $50000! All because I had generously allowed him to co-sign on the mortgage and used all the cash money from the sale of my house in Gymthorpe, to pay for the land in full, in cash. I was left to pick up the pieces of my life and rebuild both my son and my daughter. The financial separation and its ramifications were one of the hardest burdens to heal from. It still burns today, but nowhere near what it did back then.

Waiting for the criminal trial consumed our lives. It was twelve months before the trial was listed for "mention"; another two months before it was listed for the actual trial and another two months before the trial date was set down. The court process "mentions" a trial multiple times before they actually set a trial date. The "mentions" enable the court to ascertain which side is ready to proceed to trial and which side needs more time to gather evidence and develop their case. So, from the August of the previous year to the October of the following year we spent waiting to go to trial. The court system runs slowly and is such a long process.

We had endless meetings with the District Police Prosecutor to discuss what would happen at trial.

Before the trial got underway properly, Billy had to give his evidence in a recording to be played at the trial. He could do this because he was a minor. Even though he was questioned in a room and not in the court it was a traumatic experience for my 17-year-old son. He was being questioned about his own sexual habits, by Aamon's barrister, who was obviously trying to prove that an item of evidence being presented at the trial, was related to Billy and not Aamon. They were essentially accusing my son of molesting his own sister. The repercussions on Billy were immense, as he withdrew and was anxious and sullen for some months. Three months later we all had to submit to the same level of questioning.

Billy largely suffered silently in the shadows of his sister's trauma, showing a maturity beyond his years, but his day in court made the whole thing become more real in our minds.

In October of that same year, at the Ipswich District Court, the trial finally rolled around. Of the eight charges, Aamon's barrister argued away two of them before the trial even got underway. These were the two counts that happened after Courtney turned eighteen. The argument being that she could have given her consent because she was over 18 years old. How maddening, just think about that for a moment, six counts, because the court considered she could have consented even when she didn't! What an enormous slap in the face that is for a victim. It still angers me today.

Courtney was on the stand for six hours straight. When she emerged from the courtroom with my sister, who was her support person for the day, she collapsed on the floor, curled into the foetal position and sobbed, shaking uncontrollably. Aamon's family saw this reaction and just smirked at her. I had to be forcibly held back from going to her, as I was next on the stand. I was not allowed to comfort her or assist her.

It was deeply distressing and something I know other mothers would have been through. How cruel is a system that does this to its victims of crime? How much pain does it cause to be forcibly held back from comforting your daughter and having to walk into the court in that state to give your own evidence.

I spent two hours on the stand being savagely grilled by a barrister on a mission. I felt assaulted and abused, with my entire life to date being called into question; plus our sex life discussed in detail. My private pain was on display to all those sitting in the courtroom.

At one point the barrister aggressively waved a dildo in an evidence bag, at me.

I knew that the barrister was trying to label that key piece of physical evidence, provided by Courtney, as mine and not something that was used on her.

I had pieced together this clue after questioning by police and their request for our credit card statements. They had asked what I knew of a particular entry in the statement, relating to a purchase from an adult store. I responded that it was a purchase by Aamon. I had questioned him about that purchase at the time and his explanation was that he had had to buy a replacement DVD for his flat mate. When the police showed me what Aamon had actually bought, I was horrified.

The barrister kept trying to get me to change an element of my statement around our sex life. He kept suggesting that routine use of sex toys was part of our intimate lives. It wasn't, and I wasn't going to agree with him. The barrister kept aggressively rewording the question to the point I was sobbing uncontrollably on the stand, saying "no, that's not true". The judge finally cautioned the barrister.

RESILIENCE

I had done nothing wrong, yet I was made to feel like a criminal.

As I finished and left the court room, I could see the women in the jury openly crying in dismay.

My father sat white-faced, listening to it all. I will never know how he managed to sit through it all. I was hugely embarrassed that he was there, I could not look at him, but was still rather comforted just to have him there.

The rest of the week progressed in a blur of courtroom and tears. Having to see all Aamon's family everyday outside the court made our daily arrivals and departures a very painful process. They yelled verbal abuse at Courtney outside the court house, but we just tried to ignore it and kept walking. Finally, the trial finished and the jury retired to deliberate. The wait was excruciating. What seemed like hours and hours though, was merely thirty minutes.

The jury filed back in as we huddled in the front of the court room. The children and I stood, holding hands, shaking and fighting the tears that threatened to erupt at any moment. Not two metres away stood Aamon, at the defendant's desk, surrounded by his legal team. As the jury foreman made his way to the judge to deliver the verdict, Aamon broke down and started crying, turning from the desk to look directly at me.

I felt sudden panic rise in my throat. What on earth?

"Please stop," he mouthed. "I don't want to go to jail"

I was incredulous and shocked that he would think that we had any power to change anything now or stop any of the proceedings. It was too late, there was no going back now. Aamon had not shown any remorse, not one time. He had had the opportunity to plead guilty and save us all the time and pain of a trial and he hadn't. He had kept up the charade of innocence, right up until this point. Was he admitting his guilt or just scared at the possibility of going to jail? He waited until this moment to turn and beg for us to stop?

In that instant I felt completely conflicted. Here he was, about to hear the verdict and he was mouthing to me to "stop". So just as Courtney had had no power during her abuse, I hoped he felt powerless now!

I averted my face from him and watched the jury as the verdict was read. It was a deeply moving experience. Most of the women and some of the men were visibly shaken and in tears. The other men were stoic and stony-faced. I felt an overwhelming amount of compassion for them having to be part of this sordid ordeal.

In the silence of the courtroom the verdict was read.

GUILTY. GUILTY. GUILTY. GUILTY. GUILTY. GUILTY.

RESILIENCE

Guilty on all six counts of carnal knowledge of an offspring.

Of course he was, but hearing those words in the quietness of the courtroom was profound. If only I had known, this was just the beginning of our journey.

He was sentenced to four and a half years in prison for six offences of incest. It was not enough. It still seems like such an injustice. It still makes me angry to think that's all my daughter's childhood was worth.

It failed to recognise the life-long pain his crimes would create, or what he actually took from my daughter. It did not seem worthy of the amount of work that the police had to do to convict him. Even the judge describing him as "morally reprehensible" was not enough.

It was comforting however to walk towards the jury and embrace those who offered comfort, to thank them for their time and their judgement. I could see the effects such a week had had on them, they were tired, traumatised, weary and filled with compassion for us and particularly Courtney. Meanwhile Aamon was led away in handcuffs, sobbing. I felt nothing for him, no empathy, no compassion, nothing. He deserved this and more!

Courtney was still visibly shaken after listening to the verdict. She remained quiet and tight-lipped for the rest of the day.

I was surprised that the verdict did not instantly set me free from my feelings of pain and sadness. In the coming days the blackness of the world seemed to consume me. There was no happiness to be found in anything I did. I just wanted to go home and hide in my bedroom and cry. Away from the world, ashamed in my own home, shut down from life.

Life has to go on. I had to go back to work to support us. Courtney had to carry on with her life. Somehow. It was years before I learned how to nurture my own soul, how to heal the hurt and deal with the pain. I spent all my time trying to heal hers.

My new life consisted of work, home, checking on the kids, repeat. I spent my time chain smoking or sitting in a darkened lounge room with no motivation to do anything or see anyone. I drank more than was healthy and didn't eat enough to be healthy. I couldn't exercise like I used to, as I lacked the motivation to get up and go outside. My life was filled with a pervading sense of doom. There was a deep darkness that filled my soul and anger that seethed in my chest. The gravity of what I'd been through, and what I was assisting my daughter walk through, was lost on me. It was the darkest, most foreboding time in my life. I couldn't make decisions, plan from one week to the next, motivate myself. I was lost in a sea of pain and nothing much was helping.

By contrast Courtney seemed to readily get on with her life. She was desperate to prove to all concerned that she was okay. On the outside she seemed to be putting up a brave front but, on the inside, I was worried that she was not healing, just deflecting the pain. She was very cold and hostile, desperately trying to hide her pain from everyone close to her.

I also lost friends, pushed people away and was consumed by the evil of the world. It was a very bad place to be, a deep hole that I couldn't climb out of, with no one to help me. I shrivelled into a tiny former version of myself. My friend Lisa was the only one who arrived and took me to lunch, listened through my tears and encouraged me to keep going; to not give up.

I went back to work because everyone told me that's what I should do and because we needed to eat. My new colleagues showed genuine compassion and concern for my wellbeing. One of my male colleagues proved to me that there were really were wonderful decent men in the world, who cherished their wives and were in touch with their ability to be compassionate and sensitive to the needs of a vulnerable woman, such as myself. This was immensely reassuring at the time. I also discovered that one of my female work colleagues was the sister-in-law of Andrew and from her I learnt that he was now happily married with three children. I was happy to hear this news, as long as he was happy, that was wonderful. Things were slowly getting back on an even keel.

Then we were hit with horrible news.

We were advised that there would be an appeals process against Aamon's criminal conviction. Even though the appeal was submitted outside the allowable time limits, it was a landmark case, so the courts allowed it to go through.

What a slap in the face that was for all of us! The bewilderment of getting that phone call regarding the appeal and the appeal process.

I had no idea how to tell Courtney, and the very thought of having to tell her sparked panic in my chest. Then I discovered that we were not even required to be present at the appeal. We were welcome to attend but the Department of Public Prosecutors would argue the case on our behalf, in front of a panel of three Supreme Court judges.

What went down in that courtroom will remain the biggest miscarriage of justice in our lives.

Chapter

The beginning of better

"And then my soul saw you and it kind of went "Oh there you are. I've been looking for you." UNKNOWN

The road back from the horror of Aamon and the gruelling court process was long and difficult. I felt like my whole body had been turned inside out and wrung out.

A deep, dark sadness pervaded my world, stifling any joy or interest I felt in life. When I wasn't working, I spent my days in the seclusion of the house, barely functioning. I could not seem to find the sunlight in the day. I had a physical pain in my chest that felt as if it went all the way through to my soul, dragging me to the depths of despair.

The only thing tying me to the world was my children.

Courtney had found her coping mechanism. She was blocking out everything that had happened and pretending that she was doing fine. She went out and made new friends and got herself a new boyfriend. She refused to continue any sort of therapy.

However, I knew her way of coping was a façade because she was angry and upset a lot of the time and I struggled to help her deal with her emotions. She turned her back on any thoughts of university and stopped trying for any work in modelling. Her body was now desperately thin, and I worried about her physical health as much as her mental health. She worked long hours and partied and drank the rest of the time. I could see clearly the destructive patterns forming in her life but seemed unable to reach her. It was lovely to have her living at home and it was nice to be re-establishing our relationship, but she was in trouble and I knew it.

There were no further discussions about what had happened to her. She simply refused to discuss it anymore. I knew it was important that she talked to someone about what was going on in her head, but she didn't.

We went shopping and had lunch dates, co-existing in relative harmony, until her anger towards me erupted and she blamed me for what her life had become. The more I tried to get her to focus on healing herself the more she put the blame on me. I suffered from immense guilt and shame. The most distressing thing for me was seeing the loss of her dreams. I was so worried that she might remain stuck, working in a hotel, serving beer for the rest of her life, when she had had such wonderful ambitions of her modelling funding her university course. It seemed she had given up on all of that.

The fallout for Billy was equally horrendous. This once brilliant scholar completely flunked out of his final year at high school, leaving him with few of the university options that he deserved.

Billy's teachers were very understanding, but he'd had to miss so much school in his final year because of the court cases, the issues with his sister and his need for just plain time out. He wasn't even sure he wanted to go to university anymore. His beloved golf suffered as well. He went from planning a potential future as a professional golfer to refusing to go anywhere near the golf course because it reminded him of Aamon. This made me so desperately sad. I even offered to go golfing with him and pay for more professional lessons but with little success.

For six weeks after finishing school, Billy sat around the house moping and watching television, until he received an offer from his father to go and live with him in Gladstone, about five hours away from where we lived. I thought that this might be the thing Billy needed at the time although it was heartbreaking to see him go. Daniel had secured a job for Billy driving and fixing trucks. It wasn't what I wanted for him, but at least he would have a change of scenery. I didn't feel abandoned, just relieved that he would be safe with his father. I missed him desperately, and even though I talked to him on a regular basis, it wasn't the same as having him at home.

While Daniel was nurturing and supportive of Billy, he was furious with me. He blamed me for letting Aamon hurt Courtney and his recriminations were constant. I don't think he realised that I was already consumed with guilt, and even though my therapist reinforced that that I was not to blame, I still blamed myself.

Billy's stint of living with Daniel lasted six weeks and he returned home after an argument with his father. When he came home, he seemed to have lost some of the anger he was displaying before he left. When I pressed him for details of his time with his Dad, he would not say much other than he couldn't live with his father and he now understood why Daniel and I had not been able to make the marriage work. I found such depth of wisdom and understanding from my 17-year-old son astounding.

Once Billy got back to Brisbane he found work relatively quickly and set about making new friends and getting on with his life. Unlike Courtney he had managed to maintain very close friendships with his mates from Gymthorpe, a fact which no doubt sustained him through this terrible time.

We had to try to find our way through these emotional woods with the threat of Aamon's appeal hanging over us. We knew that this process would take some time and I needed to start rebuilding our lives before that, for all of our sakes.

I needed to find happiness for us all. We seemed to have had so little of it for so many years, and I knew that this was my opportunity – our opportunity - for a totally fresh start. I admit that in my eagerness to repair the damage that my choice of man – or men – had caused, I may have grasped at a few straws, but there were some good decisions too.

Firstly, I got Bella. For many years I had wanted a dog again, but Aamon had an intense dislike for dogs. Now he was gone, I thought that perhaps it was time for a puppy. Our four-legged friends are so much smarter and more intuitive than we know, and I am sure a dog would have known the evil human he was and hence his reason for not wanting one. I knew that if I started looking for a puppy the right one would let me know and that's exactly what happened.

Into my life bounced a gorgeous four-legged bundle of fluff. A Maltese/King Charles cavalier spaniel puppy; white with apricot markings and big brown eyes. In a group of four puppies she was the one who came to me and sat near me as I crouched on the floor to look at her siblings. It was she that looked up at me like she was home already and we were one.

She became my link to a glimmer of happiness. Bella seemed to know my moods. She sat on my lap while tears fell down my cheeks for hours; she slept beside my chest at night and walked with me during the day. Her big brown eyes stared into the depths of my soul and seemed to see the pain I was in; seemed to understand how healing she was and how soothing her puppy exuberance was. Her fluffy paws around my neck comforted me like no human had. She brightened the life of Courtney and Billy too, often spending her time snuggled on Billy's bed when he was home from work and then bounding up to Courtney when she came home licking her to death. She brought laughter and smiles back into our lives. Billy, in particular, responded happily to Bella's puppy kisses. Courtney kept her delight much more guarded, but when she thought no one was looking, she stooped to pat her puppy head, and rub her soft puppy ears.

I came across a group that espoused the ability to teach people how to "create health, wealth and happiness" for themselves. It looked interesting and I went along to one of their sessions. The group focused on using real estate investment to create wealth. The leader showed us places where one could find cheaper properties, do some inexpensive improvements and then use that property as an investment for the future, compounding and using the equity to purchase further properties.

He then talked about the need for self-development to build character and to be the best version of ourselves we could be. He wasn't interested in the stories of how people got to the low points in their lives, just how he could lead them into a life of abundance and happiness. It was the first time I heard someone talk about happiness being a decision. This man seemed to be the Australian version of Tony Robbins.

I booked the kids and I into a weekend retreat in the hope that we could start to heal as a family. The children were a little reluctant at first, but embraced the opportunity to spend positive time together as a family instead of rehashing all the pain we'd been thorough in recent years. The retreat was to be held in the Hunter Valley, in northern New South Wales, at a resort in the countryside, some eight hours drive from our home. It was a bonding time for all of us as we drove down, and we were all a little excited to get away and do something we had never done before.

It was an interesting journey that weekend, in which we all learnt a few new skills that have become lifelong habits.

That weekend was a bit of a breakthrough for all of us.

One of the activities we participated in was karate chopping a solid slab of pine! It was a fascinating exercise at the time, but one that we haven't repeated. This activity was achieved by singularly focusing your mind on the outcome, karate chopping the pine in half. I really did not think that I was capable of doing such a thing and thought it was ridiculous to try. But the more I listened to the instructions, the more I was able to quiet my mind and focus on the job at hand. It took me several attempts before I was able to do it, but the joy and feeling of power I got when I smashed that slab in half was imprinted on my mind forever. Billy was much quicker to achieve his split pine and Courtney was much slower, but we all did it and for the rest of the day we were unable to remove the smiles from our faces. It gave us all a sense of empowerment, strength and renewed purpose. Such a simple illustration of the power of the human mind and what we could achieve if we put our minds to it. It seemed to boost Billy and Courtney's belief in themselves exponentially.

We were also quite interested in the real estate information. We learnt what types of property to look for and in what areas of Australia, finding out that there were still properties to buy that were within even the most meagre of income levels. We all gleaned an understanding of the most important parts of the house to spend money on, and what parts could be inexpensively revamped. The retreat also covered how to spot a block of land that had the potential for subdivision; what steps to follow to subdivide the property, how to sell and market subdivided property.

We rejuvenated the family bond that remains today; learnt about focusing on actions to achieve particular results and we started to visualise our success and healing. We created our own mission statements and vision boards for the future.

The vision board was a totally new concept for me: it is basically a piece of cardboard or a large piece of paper, covered with images of all the things you want in life, from those that are materialistic in nature like cars and homes, to those things that are emotional or spiritual in nature. It's a cathartic and powerful exercise to sit with your almost adult children and talk about the dreams they have and how they intend to achieve them, with nothing standing in the way. The pictures on all our vision boards showed smiling, loving, happy relationships, with cars, homes, travel and happiness; lots of happiness.

Along with my vision board I wrote my personal mission statement. I learnt my personal mission off by heart and have used it again and again to focus my life on what's important. Here's what I wrote:

> "My mission in life is to raise my two extraordinary children to and through adulthood and to create beauty within myself and others with humility and love."

That simple statement became a mantra in the years to come and I love it now as much as I did back then.

We also had to write a small "story" on palm cards and read those each morning for the next six weeks. On my palm card I had written how I saw my life in five years' time. I wrote about healing, health and happiness. I wrote about how I wanted the children's lives to look; free from financial worry, healed, happy and thriving at life. More specifically I wrote about a fictitious man I wanted in my life, one day. He needed to be compassionate, understanding, aligned in similar values, respectful of women, highly intelligent, blond, blue-eyed, financially stable and someone who had my back.

I had a vision of a future that, at least on paper, looked good. What I didn't know is that it would take ten years to accomplish and not five. But one part of that vision would come true sooner rather than later.

Meet Paul, my knight in shining armour. I think that the universe looked down on me and decided that I had been through enough in my life at this stage and it was time for me to meet someone divinely decent.

Towards the end of that year, now sixteen months after Courtney's disclosure, I allowed myself to be talked into joining a dating website by a very dear friend.

I did not envisage a man in my life at any time in the near future but did not mind the idea of a man for company and to go out for meals with. More of a friendship than a relationship. I had made such bad choices for so long, I really did not trust myself to meet anyone suitable.

Finding a man online was probably not the best idea given my trust issues, but it did take my mind off my misery for a while, just looking to see what kind of men might be available. I met and talked with some pretty undesirable men during this time and allowed myself to go on just one date. It was horrible and I remember thinking that if this was dating via the internet, it wasn't for me. I guess that the universe had other ideas, because just as I was shutting down my profile on the dating website, an interesting message popped up on my screen and I answered it.

Paul and I talked online for a long time. Wonderful conversations flowed, and I asked all the hard questions from his views on politics, to religion, money, marriage and everything in between. It wasn't long before I realised that this was the guy I had put down on my "palm" cards, even down to the blond hair and blue eyes! He met every single criterion.

I knew I liked him a whole lot before we even met, however I was completely guarded. Paul eventually suggested we meet, and I found myself very nervous. I told him it would have to be that evening as I was leaving for a ten-day camping trip, and he agreed.

I proposed the most public place I could think of and drove to the packed cinemas in the Pacific Fair Shopping Centre on the Glitter Coast. At most, I thought I would have a nice evening with a new friend, and at worst a short dinner. I had a friend lined up to call me if I texted her a cry for help. I made sure a couple of key people knew where I was going and who I was meeting.

I was curious and in need of some normal adult conversation not punctuated by the trauma of what we had been suffering for the last couple of years. If he wasn't what he seemed, then I had a clear escape route organised and that would be the end of that.

I arrived early and wandered around window shopping and thinking that if he didn't turn up, I would be able to catch an early movie and still be home before it was too late. I had my back turned to the escalators, adjacent to the spot we had agreed to meet, and I suddenly sensed someone behind me, I slowly turned to see the most gorgeous man standing before me, smiling, with a huge bunch of flowers in his arms. I think I gasped, and my mouth dropped in wonderment. I looked over my shoulder to see if there was anyone standing behind me, assuming that the slim, closely-shaved, tanned Adonis standing before me, was looking at someone else. There was no one else there.

This man was utterly stunning and far more attractive than the profile picture I had seen, which was more than okay to begin with. I felt like I had been struck by lightning.

As we took the flowers up to the safety of my car, we started talking in the frenzied fashion of old friends catching up after a long absence. I grabbed his hand, which he graciously allowed me to do, more to steady myself than to invade his personal space. I was feeling a little intoxicated; unaccustomed to this instant and strong attraction to a man that I hardly knew. I suggested that we should go for a walk on the esplanade before deciding where to eat.

We talked for many hours that evening and walked on the beach and as we did so, my story and the trauma we had all suffered started to spill out onto the sand beneath our bare feet. We were instantly comfortable in one another's company. I thought that he would run, as fast as he could, once he heard how fractured I was and how traumatised my little family had become. Instead he listened, quietly and compassionately, before explaining that he and his family had gone through something similar with his sister and his paternal grandfather. I was more and more amazed by this man; the more I learned, the more amazed I became. How could I be so lucky? How was this guy not married with kids and an equally beautiful wife? What had transpired to bring us together on this hot December night on the Glitter Coast?

By 11 pm I knew I had to get home, to be on my way camping first thing in the morning, so we walked in silence up to the parked cars. I did not want to leave. It had been such a memorable night. As I went to unlock the door of my car, before saying goodbye, Paul asked if he could kiss me good night. I had been a teenager the last time someone showed me enough respect to ask me, before kissing me. I was now over 40 years old and this was so unexpected. I, of course, said, "Yes."

That kiss turned my world upside down. The depth, powerfulness and deliciousness of that kiss had me in tears on the drive home, at the magnitude of what had just happened. Now I wouldn't see him for ten days.

I need not have worried. A day later he rang and the friends I was camping with encouraged me to invite him along too.

Double Island Point on the Sunshine Coast, Queensland, is a camping spot only accessible by four-wheel-drive, so my friends gladly arranged to drive to the ferry to pick Paul up to join us. My friends where camping experts and we had a camping shower, solar hot water and a toilet. Our tents were pitched under the shade of the she-oaks at the edge of the nature reserve.

The next few days were spent in this idyllic, pristine location, twenty meters from the water. The Queensland, December sun bore down on us as we swam and caught fish off the beach. Hammocks swung in the trees for relaxing afternoons spent sleeping and reading. At night we sat around glorious beach bonfires, talking about everything from politics to children.

For the first time in more than five years I started to feel the tension ebb from my shoulders, as I enjoyed the company of friends and the easy company and conversation of Paul. I laughed and finally started to relax.

Paul was younger than me and although he'd had long term relationships before, these had not progressed to marriage. Paul liked to tell everyone he had been waiting for me, but behind this lovely line was an emotionally mature decision he had made years ago. Paul decided that because of what had happened to his sister he did not want to have kids of his own and he did not really want his surname to be passed onto future generations. I understood this reasoning and it made me respect him even more.

Paul had a well-paid job in Brisbane where he worked hard as a computer engineer and had paid off his own home some years earlier so was financially stable. He used his home as a weekend escape and rented an apartment close to the sea on Burleigh Beach so he could surf each morning. Being with him was so easy, there was a distinct absence of angst of any kind. He thought I was easy going, I thought he was easy to talk to. Other than surfing, he loved to ride his bike and had participated in many long rides to raise money for various charities. He was quiet, respectful and he listened to what everyone said. He was like my other half, my soul mate and we knew it from very early on.

We became inseparable.

It was fortuitous that we had that first month to ourselves, as both of us had annual leave which coincided with the New Year period and January. The kids were off with friends and family and we could take our time getting to know each other. We did not share our new relationship with anyone until after this time. The repercussions of me being in a new relationship provoked a backlash from my family and some of my friends which was vicious. Luckily, by this stage I had started to have more confidence in my own decisions, made on my own terms. Paul was a good decision and I was not going to let anyone destroy something so beautiful before it had the time to grow and mature.

Courtney was the most vocal in the family regarding my new relationship. She had every right to be, seeing as my past decisions in terms of relationships had ended up being so poor. She rained down nasty vitriol on my head, reminiscent of the worst of times after her disclosure. Her pain was still so raw and always directed straight at me and I took it at that time, because there were still lingering thoughts of unworthiness and guilt in my mind.

Later In therapy I learnt how to listen and not condone this type of behaviour from her. In the halcyon days after meeting Paul, her words cut me like a knife and left me battered and bruised emotionally for days. It would be years before she recognised the pattern of her behaviour herself. Until then I just took whatever it was that was meted out.

She wasn't jealous that I had found someone new, because Courtney was also dating anew, albeit a particularly narcissistic young man with delusions of grandeur. This guy was a real estate salesman, high on self-importance, but low on manners, and he had obviously decided that because he was dating my daughter, he could say what he wanted and do whatever he wanted in my house. Between the two of them, there were many times I just wanted to run away, to get away from their constant barrage of criticism and immature insights, not backed up by reality, or send them away. They both said that I should not be dating again; that it was selfish of me to even consider bringing another man into the house, given what had happened to Courtney.

This view was generally held by the rest of my family for some time, as well. It may have been Aamon who committed the crime, but I was the one being held accountable for his sins.

How Paul remained calm and positive throughout this terrible time is testament to the incredible man that he is. For the first time in my whole life I had a rock to lean on. It was a comforting and liberating experience.

The appeal trial arrived in the February of the year following the criminal trial. Paul and I attended the Supreme Court for the first Court of Appeal trial, despite being told that we did not need to. We listened to arguments by the district prosecutor and Aamon's barrister. We were not allowed to interject, respond or be involved in this court procedure in any way. We had to sit at the back of the courtroom and just listen. It was torture. The case was at the mercy of a district prosecutor who stated to the court that she had not had adequate time to prepare for this appeal, but that she was happy to proceed anyway and the court let her. She may not have had time to prepare, but she certainly didn't advocate for Courtney.

The legal argument in the appeals court was complex and legally technical. The Appeal had been granted because the law under which Aamon had been tried and convicted, was brand new and controversial. The state wanted to treat any sexual abuse of minors in a family setting as equally reprehensible, even if the adult was not their real parent or step-parent, but rather a defacto parent as in Aamon's case. He had brought Courtney and Billy up with me since they were young and therefore was a father figure to them.

That is why he had been charged with "Carnal knowledge of an offspring" even though those words did not really apply, as far as most people understood them. But the new law specifically included the children of one's partner, living under the same roof.

In the first Court of Appeal trial Aamon's defence lawyer pointed out that when the sexual acts were taking place with Courtney, the law didn't even exist, so how was his client supposed to know he was breaking the law.

The judges seemed to accept this.

He then argued that Courtney was over the age of consent on all the counts Aamon had been convicted for, and the evidence indicated that the carnal knowledge was consensual, therefore legal.

My anger overflowed at that point, but Paul held me back from standing and shouting at the judges, as the defence lawyer highlighted to the court that Courtney had herself said: "I just lay there and let it happen." I wanted to scream at them: "What was she supposed to do? Haven't you heard of grooming and psychological manipulation in these crimes. It was a constant onslaught."

Instead I remained silent and watched the judges pondering this statement. In my mind I knew how despondent Courtney had become, and NOT how accepting the court was portraying her.

The defence lawyer concluded that even though Aamon's actions were morally reprehensible, they were not unlawful at the very time they were committed, even if they were now.

At no time did the District Prosecutor intervene to correct these notions.

By way of a compromise, the defence barrister suggested that Aamon did not deserve to be in prison, and that the prison term was too long, and should be suspended. He detailed all that he had lost as a result of his conviction and asked for his conviction to be lessened to eighteen months and suspended thereafter, although his criminal conviction would still stand.

This was bad enough, but then the District Prosecutor stood and acknowledged that Courtney was over the age of consent for the crimes detailed, and even though she was living in a defacto family situation with Aamon, she would have been legally entitled to marry him once she turned eighteen, so if the sexual intercourse was consensual, then the sexual assault convictions for after she was an adult would not stand. She said three of the six counts should therefore be quashed. I was watching the entire case against Aamon unravelling before my eyes. It didn't seem real.

The matter was held over pending further legal discussion and further submissions from the defence barrister and we were told we could leave. I was shattered, and Paul was beyond astounded that this was happening. We had no idea what to do or where to turn. We did not tell Courtney in the vague hope that the second court of appeal would do what the first had not done.

When the case went back to court we were not notified. The only way I was able to determine what happened during that trial was via court transcripts. It was equally confusing that the terms of carnal knowledge and incest were used interchangeably throughout the court of appeals transcripts.

In the second appeal trial, the judges agreed that Aamon's crimes did not constitute the general understanding of "incest" at the time, and they accepted that Aamon was having consensual intercourse with Courtney!

There was a general discussion around a retrial on other charges, but the defence team insisted because the three charges related to when Courtney was 18 years old had already been quashed, that information would taint a trial on the three counts of sexual abuse when she was aged 16-18. It was therefore decided it was better to just throw out the remaining three charges too.

I couldn't believe what I was reading.

This led to further legal argument around Aamon's release from prison and bail conditions. The District Prosecutor stated that she would not impose bail conditions. They then started discussing what to do with Aamon. The defence team wanted him released immediately. The District Prosecutor said she wouldn't impose any bail conditions. So Aamon was free to be released from jail, after serving only four and a half months and all his convictions were to be quashed with no criminal record. His name would be removed from the Sex Offenders' Registry. There was no definitive decision on if or when a retrial would happen

We had no recourse to appeal, as it was a criminal case and not a civil one. Writing about it now is as devastating as living through it was back then.

I remember the day I took the phone call from the Ipswich District court prosecutor, full of apology and disbelief. I almost dropped the phone, such was the shock that engulfed me that day. I had to leave work, unable to focus for the rest of the day, desperately unsure of how I would tell Courtney what had happened. I wanted to hurt Aamon, I wanted to hurt the defence barrister who had gotten him out of jail. I was seething with pain and anger and dismay, shaking with disbelief.

Later that afternoon I called Courtney, asking her to come home as I had something important I needed to talk to her about. I sat her down in the lounge, looked her in the eye and explained that they had just let Aamon out of jail. The look of horror on her face will forever be etched in my memory. She screamed and yelled, punched the lounge, and then sobbed in big gulping tears. I tried to talk about the practicalities of his release and how we should protect her going forward, but she wasn't listening. I just watched her die a little more inside that day, saw any healing that had happened seep from her. She withered a little more, became more sullen and colder. She had been brave, had trusted herself to the system and the system had let her down. Courtney changed her name, changed her phone number and moved out of the house!

Courtney and her boyfriend, the real estate guy, moved from Springfield Lakes to inner Brisbane, where Courtney found a job with the state tolls office. I don't think her relationship was progressing very well but she only confided snippets of information to me, from time to time. She had by this stage given up any idea of going to university and had stopped seeking modelling work entirely. Her boyfriend would turn out to be a real problem in her life and eventually after a physical altercation, she did leave him and return home.

Billy by this stage had found some cold calling work with an electricity company in Brisbane and had also moved out. He too, had dismissed any idea of going to university. I missed his company, but it was good for him to start to live life as a young adult. Before too long he met a really nice girl and they moved into together. Billy seemed to thrive in a steady job, with a steady girlfriend. We spoke every other day and he seemed to be much older and wiser than his older sister. He managed to have a good relationship with his father once he was no longer living with him, and he and his girlfriend would drive up to see him when they had the time and the money.

Paul eventually moved into my house in Springfield Lakes and life started to settle just a little bit. There were still weekly recriminations from Courtney, plus endless phone calls and text messages about everything that was happening in her life. Although she made it clear that she resented me, she made it equally obvious she still needed me. Paul stayed patiently in the background of the children's lives, only offering opinions when asked. He was, however my back up, my confidante and my listening post, whilst I tried to sort through the morass that was my life.

Courtney still refused to have any form of regular counselling and her drinking and drug taking started to escalate after yet another short-term broken relationship with another young man. There were also numerous, half-hearted attempts to take her own life, from alcoholic poisoning, to calling me stating she was about to end it all by taking a drug overdose, to slashing her wrists. Each time I talked her out of it or down; whatever I needed to do to ease her pain in that moment. It was a harrowing for me and distressing for her. She was in a world of pain and didn't let anyone close any more. She was stuck in her pain until she recognised her need for deeper healing and began to understand her trauma. She distanced herself from my sister and my mother and father, whom she had been so close to. She was shutting down, putting up the barriers so no one could ever hurt her again.

She was not close to her real father. He had not made any attempt to contact her or even help her in any way, despite me begging for him to call her. Courtney was not close to Daniel and fought with his second wife and their three children. She would not discuss anything with Paul, not that I expected her to.

I loved her unconditionally and demonstrated that love as often as I could. I told her every day that no matter what she did, I would not desert her. That little statement proved to be the most powerful thing in finally setting her free. I stubbornly clung to the hope that a mother's love would be enough to heal her hurt. But as powerful as a mother's love is, there comes a time when you have to do the work required to heal your own hurt.

Paul and I decided to make a sea-change, literally, and move from outside Brisbane to the Glitter Coast, about 45 minutes' drive away. A move to the Glitter Coast, where Paul could be closer to the surfing he loved and the tranquillity we desperately sought. It seemed like the ideal solution to draw a line under the past and forge a new beginning. The house in Springfield Lakes had so many memories; at times it was like living in the house of the damned, with all those bad memories constantly reinforced. All the financial strain of the last few years had abated and the rising equity in the home now meant we were able to purchase in the more expensive Glitter Coast real estate market.

We looked for a rural property first, in the hinterland around the Glitter Coast. I found a perfect block, only to discover it was completely out of our price range and we ended up settling for a lovely renovated home close to the water, backing onto a nature reserve and beside a vacant nature park. This would be a new start for Paul and I where we would create new memories of our own. With both children now independent, I felt like we were moving into the childfree years of pre-retirement.

The birds and wildlife sounds which greeted us each morning from the nature reserve calmed my soul. It was almost as good as living in the countryside. Walking and bike riding in and around our home proved to be the solace I needed to heal and as I started some intensive therapy, it provided an outlet for the anguish of my soul. Courtney had another relationship break-up and wanted to move home to join us.

I was nervous about her coming to live with us again, not wanting to step back into the battle zone home life had been before she moved out, but we reluctantly agreed. We did set some ground rules; no drugs, no binge drinking and she had to see a therapist once a week. She agreed.

With Courtney back at home and a new corporate role for me on the Glitter Coast, I was back in testing waters again. The constant feeling of being on edge had returned and the initial solace I found living on the Glitter Coast evaporated. The stress of living with Courtney was immense, but I saw no alternative except to keep on helping and assisting her where I could. Her issues eroded my levels of coping ability and increased my stress cup to overflowing. I had a script constantly playing in my head that said I was the saviour of her soul and she was not going to be an abuse statistic.

Sometime after Courtney had moved back in with us, and a short time into my new full-time role, which was causing me so much stress, I had a second breakdown. I did not think it was possible to have another breakdown after being put on medication and having therapy, but the second breakdown taught me a lot more in terms of self-management and coping mechanisms. I was at a point where tears were again just beneath the surface and I felt the blackness descending. This time I feared what was coming; this time I knew I needed help and fast. I didn't get it fast enough to avoid it all together, but some people like myself are slow learners.

Paul was the first to notice. He found me one night after work sitting quietly crying in the lounge room. It had been a tough day, struggling with new personalities and a workload I was very unfamiliar with. A colleague at work had confided in me, saying she had just found a brother she never knew she had. I had listened and tried to suggest some coping strategies to assist her, but she verbally attacked me, saying "you have no idea what pain is" and "how could you even remotely understand what I am going through?" When I started to tell her that I did understand more than she could know, she derided my "wonderful life" and "no knowledge of family trauma". Then she burst into tears and asked me to leave. I did, and she left for the day and went home sick. I continued my day but cried all the way home. When I got home, I couldn't stop the tears, no matter how hard I tried.

Paul insisted I went to the doctor and took the day off to make sure I did. To hear the words "you're having another breakdown" sent shockwaves through my heart and distressed me even further. I had to immediately stop work again, increase my medication and see a psychiatrist for formal diagnosis. I later learned that trauma leaves indelible marks on your brain and changes the way you think. I needed to treat myself more compassionately and change the way I thought and reacted to life.

The psychiatrist agreed that my current medication was no longer working and that we needed to try something else. The new medication came with a raft of side effects including weight gain, loss of libido and increased hunger. I did not want this diagnosis, I felt like my mind had let me down - again. This time I was more determined than ever to research every option and to understand what I needed to do to heal myself and to make sure it did not happen again. The five years since the first breakdown had taught me a lot but I had so much more to learn in terms of nurturing my soul, listening to my body, understanding my diagnosis and living with depression and anxiety rather than letting it rule my life.

It took me quite a while to find a therapist who was able to engage with me on an intellectual and therapeutic level. It took months, working through the emotional pain, to get to the point where my exhausted mental self could start to move on.

I saw Maddie twice a week to begin with, then as her strategies started to work, weekly, then fortnightly and so on. She effectively and permanently helped me change my thinking from a negatively-charged internal dialogue to a positive one. It is she who actively encouraged me to write about all my experiences, it was she who applauded the success of my current relationship with Paul.

It was my therapist Maddie who constructively helped me to manage the behaviour issues in Courtney's life. She who was the holder of my most intense and painful moments, the keeper of my secret delusions and unchallenged thought patterns. My therapist, my confidante, my friend.

She allowed me to grieve for the loss of my wedding to Aamon without judgement. I had never allowed myself to grieve for the loss of what I had hoped for, or mourn a future that was taken from me. All the while Paul supported me through this process, encouraged me, loved me even when I was not the partner he deserved.

I had held onto much of the memorabilia from that aborted wedding. I still had the wedding dress, all the decorations, the plans, the receipts. Part of my healing started with getting rid of those items. I cried deep, hiccupping tears of betrayal the day I gave my beautiful Elizabeth DeVargo designer wedding gown away. It was so elegant and perfect – the pale blush colouring, beading and draping that had come from a concept in my head. When I let go of it, I finally let go of the idea of ever being married again. I certainly would not have worn the gown ever again, there was too much pain associated with it.

To an outsider this must seem bizarre, why did I have such an attachment to such an angst-ridden relationship? But I did love Aamon, for all the bad in him there was also charm and I was deeply committed to him, so much so that it had blinded me to his dark side.

I burnt many of the other bits and pieces from that ill-fated wedding but kept my visual diary. My visual diary was a notebook that held all the elements and concepts I had planned for the wedding celebration; different ideas; colour schemes, clippings from magazines and newspapers with wedding ideas. I kept it not to hold onto the past, but to remind me of the future; as a visual acknowledgment of the pain I had been through and survived.

During the recovery from the second breakdown, my anxiety went into overdrive. I experienced panic attacks that were completely debilitating. I knew it was all the negative energy coming out, and I knew that it needed to, but when your body shaking uncontrollably it is a horrid sensation and you feel so weak. I was a shaking, fearful mess of tears and emotions.

At that time my mother's brother passed away. He was the alcoholic abuser and perpetrator of sin who had abused some of his sisters and was rumoured to have hurt his own children. Regardless, most of my mother's family were going to attend, and my mother wanted me to go too. Clearly, I was really too ill to be attending the funeral of such a horrid man, but as usual, despite all the advances I had made, I thought that I should do as my mother suggested.

My uncle had succumbed to oesophageal cancer and had died trying to clear his blocked tracheotomy with a biro, a bizarrely macabre death. I secretly thought that this was a fitting death for such a reprehensible man.

I did not go to the actual ceremony, but arrived for the wake. As I walked in, I felt my body start to shake and tears start to form in my eyes. I tried to walk back out but was embraced by several members of the family who had not realised my distress. It was my father who suddenly came to my rescue. He grabbed me, led me by my arm and walked me away from the gathering. As I was shaking and gulping for air, he quietly held my hand, instructing me to breathe, saying that he was there and that I was going to be okay. In that moment, after all that had happened between us, I knew that he understood; knew what I was going through, and I knew that he loved me. It took half an hour for my body to settle down and hours for my brain to calm, but just having my Dad by my side, understanding, made all the world of difference.

I was getting better slowly, but Courtney was not on the same trajectory. She had begun mixing in some very worrying company, with the members of an outlawed motorcycle gang on the Glitter Coast, the Finks. She was "seeing" one of them who had been imprisoned for the murder of a "Hells Angel" rival in a brawl. Three men were shot, and three men were stabbed and the man my daughter was seeing had served six and a half years in jail. The brawl had colloquially been dubbed the "Ballroom Blitz"

I decided to try and proactively "manage" the situation without trying to tell her what to do. I said I wanted to meet him and talk to him. Nothing much scares me, so until I knew more about him I resolved to treat her choice with kindness and compassion. Into our dining room walked this mammoth, tattooed biker, incongruously dressed in a suit. He was quite a good-looking guy and softly spoken. Paul had disappeared, wanting no part of the meeting and not even approving of this man being in our home.

We shook hands and I asked him to take a seat at the table. I wanted to look him in the eye as I asked him his intentions with Courtney. Yes, I did ask him exactly that! He spoke calmly and respectfully, saying he appreciated being allowed into our home, as many would not be so generous. I then looked him in the eye and stated that if he hurt my daughter or caused her pain in anyway, I knew where he lived, and I would remove his testes. It was laughable really, but I meant it. He smiled and nodded, saying that if he did indeed hurt her, I was welcome to them. He left after giving me a hug.

All too soon, he did break Courtney's heart, not so badly as to create lasting pain and embarrassment, but enough for her to consider that she had better options.

When it happened, I did remind him over Facebook message that he indeed owed me those parts of his anatomy. He said if I could find him that night, I was definitely entitled to them. This led to a conversation about his upbringing, prison and his mum. He thanked me for listening and treating him with kindness. He thought I was a "badass" Mum and that he wasn't good enough for my daughter. I was left with a deep feeling of sadness towards him and for him.

There was another dalliance with danger for Courtney which had rather worse consequences for her. Another bikie associate introduced her to cocaine. Despite our rule of no drugs, she disregarded our request and it was to her detriment. This man treated her so appallingly that I feared for her life. Her subsequent drug addiction was powerful and drove her poor decision making for months. The worst part was the realisation that she was in so deep, so quickly and it took a while for me to acknowledge it for what it was, despite the evidence before my eyes; the not coming home until dawn; sleeping all day and deeply-reddened soulless eyes that greeted me whenever I saw her.

Paul questioned Courtney, but she denied she was taking drugs. We then had an early morning visit from the federal police. It was not my first police raid, but it was Paul's. The bursting through the door, the yelling and shouting, guns drawn was scarier than the last time. They demanded to know where Courtney was, where Paul was and where the drugs were hidden. They searched the house and didn't find anything, but they were angry, mean and obnoxious. They demanded we call Courtney and then they summoned her home from work.

I was so on edge that Courtney was being interviewed by police again and under terrifying circumstances. In the end we suggested that we needed to talk to a lawyer and that she would agree to an interview the next day at the police station, provided I could accompany her. With legal advice under our belts Courtney made a statement to police indicating that she had no knowledge of any cocaine importation, which had been the premise of the raid in the first place.

After this raid Courtney tried again to take her own life. It was the worst attempt for me to discover. She had come home, drunk and stoned. I gave her some water and settled her into bed with Panadol, deftly avoiding the argument she was attempting to have with me. I sat with her until I thought she had fallen asleep, then I went back to our room to toss and turn. Somewhere in the moments between being asleep and awake, I heard a strange noise coming from the garage. I sat bolt upright in bed. It sounded like someone was trying to break in. I crept out to investigate.

I can still see the rope and the belt attached to the garage hoist in the ceiling of the carport. Courtney was sitting on the ground outside. I looked in disbelief and horror as alarm shot through my chest. I felt like everything moved in slow motion as I looked at Courtney. Her reddened eyes, dilated pupils, wide-eyed look and marks on her neck which confirmed my worst fears. I struggled to get her up and inside for some coffee, where she tearfully explained that she couldn't even "off" herself properly. The belt had slipped and released her neck before any damage could be done.

Somewhere in her description she managed a wry laugh and then I laughed too, not at her but at the incongruity of our lives and what we had become. We actually laughed. Somehow, in that moment, I got through to her that life was worth living, that I was there for her and never going to leave her. I understood that she just wanted the horrible, debilitating pain to stop; just wanted life to stop hurting so god darn much and for the ache in her heart to cease. I told her she was going to be okay, perhaps not now, but soon and that laughter would enter our lives again. She would be happy, I promised.

I tucked her back into bed and slipped out to remove the rope and belt before Paul realised what had transpired during the night.

After that night, Paul and I sat Courtney down and demanded she seek help. She had nowhere to go, no friends that she trusted, no family that were capable of helping her, except us. However hard it was to say, Paul and I insisted that if she continued with the drug taking, she would have to pack up and leave now, because it was destroying her and we did not want to watch that happen. We told her she had to cut all ties with any motorcycle gang members, get a job, pay some rent and help around the house. To our huge surprise she agreed.

She also agreed to weekly therapy sessions with a new counsellor, and to random drug testing if we suspected anymore drug use. We even got her to sign a contract with our expectations of her detailed in writing.

It was the beginning of her recovery.

Chapter

The long way back

"Before you heal the body, you must first heal the mind" ARISTOTLE

Most people associate depression with a feeling of sadness, with tears and melancholy. But for many of the one million Australian adults living with the condition, it is actually a complete absence of feeling; a crippling apathy.

I remember in an attempt to break myself out of my own doom and gloom, I booked Paul and I onto a hot air balloon ride. It was something we had always wanted to do and I thought it might be a fun way to spend a Sunday morning.

We arrived at the balloon launch rendezvous in the pre-dawn darkness. The balloons were already making a bright splash in the sky. The crisp early morning air was filled with the smell of the gas used to inflate the sleeves. Although I had arranged it, I was finding it hard to get into the spirit of the morning. I was going through the motions. I think Paul enjoyed it, and I hope he didn't notice the emptiness in me, but I fear he did, and I realised how much my past was impacting on my present; how impossible it was proving for me to bring myself back from what had happened, let alone for Courtney. At least we had some beautiful photos to remind me of the day, even if my senses were dulled and my excitement diminished.

It was another catalyst for me to acknowledge and understand that living in the moment and remaining in the moment, are important components of human resilience. I was reminded that happiness is a conscious decision and that I needed to focus my mind on being happy, for there was so much in life to be happy about. Despite the issues that we all faced, I needed to take more time to enjoy moments of happiness, concentrating on the present and enjoying the wonderful life I had.

Courtney seemed to be making positive strides towards true healing. She had a good part-time job at an upmarket restaurant about five minutes from home. She was attending therapy regularly and going to gym sessions as well. She had stopped drinking so much and the drug use had completely gone. She maintained a few close girlfriends who kept her company given she was no longer dating anyone. Paul and I decided that it might be time for a long overdue holiday for the two of us.

We chose a cruise up the east coast of Australia, into Indonesia, and around various ports in South East Asia, including Thailand, Vietnam and Cambodia.

One night after a perfect dinner on board, Paul suggested we walk the upper decks of the boat to enjoy the moonlit night. I was contemplating the beauty of the stars, leaning against the railing when he suddenly dropped to one knee and asked if I would consider being his wife.

I gasped and heard myself saying "yes, yes, yes". He presented me with the most beautiful ring I had ever seen; a huge antique-looking blood red garnet, surrounded by champagne and brown diamonds in a setting of rose gold. All the stones had been sourced from Australian mines. Of course, every time I look at the ring now, I am reminded of that extremely romantic moment. Now I knew what happiness meant. I was happier than I had ever been, and it was a wonderfully delicious feeling.

I returned home on cloud nine and this time the children seemed genuinely happy to hear our news.

I had another wedding to plan, although we had given ourselves twelve months to get it right. We wanted something small, simple and elegant with lots of family.

At this time, I was entitled to a pay-out from my work superannuation fund if I was unable to return to work due to the anxiety and depression symptoms, or I could continue with the weekly payments for another six months.

My doctor and my therapist advised me to take the lump sum and stay off work, to just focus on getting better and avoiding all stress. It was not something I was comfortable with as I had always worked and provided for my family, but it was, without a doubt the best decision I ever made. I continued to get better and I was always around to help Courtney when she needed me. I had settled my priorities.

I started to see the joy in things again and was feeling relaxed and content with the wedding just on the horizon. But then, all of a sudden I started to feel very tired. I was finding it difficult to stay awake past early evening and I never wanted to get up in the morning. Then I got searing burning pain in my hands and my feet, making it difficult to walk or hold anything.

At the time I thought that I had contracted some type of viral illness and Paul insisted that I see a doctor. I had only just hobbled through the door of the doctor's office when he said: "You have Rheumatoid Arthritis." The diagnosis floored me. I had a swathe of blood tests and x-rays which confirmed it. I knew little about the disease itself, other than it had a genetic component, but was often triggered by trauma or illness. I guessed I had the traumatic component covered, but I also knew the genetic component came from my father's side. His cousins and two of his aunts had the disease.

So began my battle with Chronic Aggressive Rheumatoid Arthritis. In the first instant, the specialist hoped that a round of medication would force the disease into remission, however mine refused to read the memos about this and fought the medication on every front, proving that it wasn't going to leave my body without a fight. For anyone managing a chronic illness, they will know the pain of not only the disease process, but the constant rounds of doctors and specialist appointments, weekly blood tests, x-rays, scans, eye tests, skin checks and so on. Rheumatoid Arthritis is a beast of a disease, and it would take my sole focus to learn to live with it and manage its debilitating effects. But I didn't want to cancel another wedding and I had a honeymoon to enjoy.

In the lead up to the wedding Paul did something for me that helped my self esteem exponentially. He paid for beautiful new veneers for of all my front teeth, top and bottom. What a gift! At least now, when I smiled, it was with a mouth full of white teeth. The difference this made to me was enormous and every time I look at those lovely white teeth, I am filled with gratitude and a sense of wonderment at the difference they made.

Paul and I were married on an Island off the Gold Coast, at sunset on a beautiful autumn evening. To say it was the happiest day of my life was an understatement. Courtney as my bridesmaid and Paul had Billy as his groomsman. Courtney and I spent the morning getting our hair and makeup done before boarding a catamaran for the journey to the island. It was such a magical afternoon. I was getting married with my children's blessing and that felt wonderful.

The guests were taken by boat to the island and were there waiting for our arrival. I had secretly organised a helicopter to take Billy and Paul to the ceremony. We have amazing photos of the two of them beaming out of the helicopter windows at take-off and set down. I remember feeling like I was floating as I walked up the beach on the arm of my father, towards the sea side chapel, with tears of happi-ness beading in my eyes. Our heartfelt, self-penned humorous vows and ceremony had everyone in stitches as well as tears. It was such a joyful ceremony, so filled with love and promise.

I walked down the aisle to Christina Perri's song "A thousand years" which seemed particularly fitting.

>We danced our first wedding dance to Beyoncé's "Halo"
>SONGWRITERS: BEYONCE KNOWLES/EVAN KIDD BOGART/RYAN B. TEDDER HALO LYRICS © SONY/ATV MUSIC PUBLISHING LLC, DOWNTOWN MUSIC PUBLISHING

We had taken dance lessons so we could surprise everyone with our polished wedding dance, but we had forgotten to practice with the wedding dress on, and we ended up doing a funny side-step that barely resembled what we had practiced. It didn't matter one bit, as we laughed the whole way through anyway. Even writing about our wedding day now is giving me a wonderful giddy feeling; a happy bubble of delight rising in my chest and making me grin from ear to ear. It was such a great day.

Our wonderful wedding was only topped by our honeymoon in the Maldives. The breathtaking beauty of the island archipelago took our breath away. We spent a week in an overwater bungalow, with steps down to the warm, clear waters. We snorkelled for hours at a time, exploring the reefs in and around our bungalow. The brightly-coloured fish, sharks and coral enthralled us each day. We went deep sea fishing, island hopping and dolphin spotting and just enjoyed our magical, happy bubble.

When we got home, there was more to celebrate before long. Courtney met someone who lived just across the road from us. A neighbour arrived one afternoon to introduce himself while she was washing her car.

Jett was a good-looking young man and it wasn't long before he was taking Courtney out and spoiling her with thoughtful gifts and his undivided attention.

Paul and I were nervous for our girl, but he said all the right things, made all the right gestures. The only cloud on the horizon was his behaviour when he was drunk, when he would put Courtney down and argue with her. We realised Courtney had to make her own decisions, but when your child has been through such an emotional battering it is hard not to want to wrap her in cotton wool.

We made it clear to Jett that Courtney needed calm and happiness, but he could still make life difficult from time to time.

They moved in to Jett's house together. I wasn't all that happy with this arrangement, but at least Courtney was close enough to pop over to see us and we were close enough to help her out if she needed us to. She also decided to go back to university which was a great development.

Billy and his long-term girlfriend had moved into a little unit by themselves and Billy too, had started to think about applying for university. His girlfriend was studying massage therapy and Billy decided he wanted to do a physiotherapy degree. Some of his friends were physiotherapists and so was his uncle in Canada, so he knew what it entailed. Because he had done so poorly in his senior year of high school, he had to do a number of bridging courses before he could even apply for admission into university.

Paul was able to help tutor Billy in chemistry and physics to satisfy the prerequisites of the course. Eventually, due to the competition for admission to the physiotherapy degree courses, Billy settled for a first degree in Exercise Physiology, which he passed with honours.

He then went on to do one year of a physiotherapy master's degree before finally getting into a brilliant university to study a Doctorate of Physiotherapy.

Whilst all this was happening, my battle with Rheumatoid Arthritis was intensifying. The disease was failing to respond to popular and proven medication regimes and was making life extremely painful and uncomfortable for me. I researched some of the more natural methodology in search of healing strategies for my body. I found that twice weekly Pilates helped, along with a change in diet, homeopathic remedies and hydrotherapy. The one thing I struggled with the most was the reduction of stress and worry in my life.

Soon we would find a solution that helped on many fronts.

Chapter Ten

Life Resilience

"Persistence and resilience only come from having been given the chance to work through difficult problems." GEVER TULLEY

Paul and I began to talk about moving again, staying close to the Glitter Coast, but living out in the hinterland, which we hadn't been able to afford before. We wanted more space, the ability to breathe country air but still be close to the beach. We wanted more animals too. It was also hoped that the quiet, stress free, county life would help with managing my Rheumatoid Arthritis. Courtney seemed pretty settled into life with Jett and they seemed to be making their relationship work. Paul and I still had our reservations about Jett, but Courtney seemed happy, so we kept it to ourselves.

I looked at property and land around the hinterland. Nothing interested me until I came across the block of land we had looked at four years before. Here it was for sale again, at half the price it was originally advertised for. It was a beautiful three and a half acres with an additional acre of land adjacent to the creek. The elderly owner of the block was selling due to his age. It was his favourite block and the only one left in the original subdivision. He wasn't about to sell it to just anyone.

The owner wanted to meet us and know exactly what our plans for the block were. We talked about building a small house, having some goats, chickens, ducks, a vegetable garden and increasing the size of the existing orchard, so that we could live sustainably and provide an oasis for the family to visit and for the grandkids one day. He seemed delighted with our answer and suggested we put an offer in writing to him.

Much to our surprise, he accepted our offer and we started the process of purchasing the block, refinancing and searching for a home builder.

With the purchase finalised, we started planting trees all around the perimeter of the block. Many happy weekends were spent mowing and gardening, camping in the big old shed already on the block, barbequing dinner and camp fires at night. Wonderful, new memories were created in that time of dreaming, planning and gardening.

Before we started building our home, Courtney fell pregnant. I had mixed emotions as I knew by this stage that she was not as happy in the relationship as she had been. She had just finished the first year of a university degree and I wondered how a baby would fit into this environment. We spent a lot of time talking about parenthood and how hard it can be. Unfortunately, she miscarried the baby before the end of the first trimester, making her relieved and sad in equal measures.

We went on to start the definitive planning for the new home. We knew that it had to be a highset home due to the potential of some flooding water across the property.

As there were no flood maps in existence, we went back to the owner for advice on the height of the home to be safely out of flood water. We all agreed that the house needed to be above the height level of the highest rung on the bridge three hundred meters from the building site. Height determined, we proceeded with the design of the home and commenced building.

Moving to the freedom and serenity of the Tranquil Valley was one of the best decisions of our lives. The property is a place of spiritual healing, serenity and peace. I found all the gardening a wonderful form of therapy and escapism. We increased the size of the orchard from a few citrus trees to include a plethora of fruit trees, berries and vines. I also put in a topical garden on the protected side of the old large shed growing bananas, mangos, paw paw and passionfruit. We set up raised vegetable gardens to grow vegetables, protecting them from the chickens and ducks.

We purchased our first goats Whiskey, Snoopy and Cuddles, closely followed by two llamas, Avocado and Apu Moche. The joy that of all of this imparted into our lives was enormous and I began to experience that deep wonderful, whole of body happiness and contentedness. I felt like I could finally breathe and my chest no longer hurt.

About three months after Courtney's miscarriage, she fell pregnant again after a course of antibiotics. She continued working and studying part time at university until the birth of the baby. Her relationship with Jett was still plagued with issues, as Courtney had not yet learnt to put boundaries around herself and Jett had a problem with drugs and alcohol. We tried to assist in helping them navigate their relationship, but many times we pulled away in the hope that they would be able to negotiate the issues themselves. I was beyond excited to know that Courtney and Jett were expecting a baby boy and everyone happily anticipated the birth of this much loved baby.

Courtney went into labour at 10.30pm the day before her due date. I fully expected that, as it was her first baby, she would be in for a long labour. I got a phone call at 2.30am early the next morning, asking me to get to the hospital.

I jumped out of bed, so excited to know I was about to meet our new grandbaby but also worried about how Courtney was managing her labour pain.

I arrived at the hospital just in the nick of time, with Courtney ready to push and deliver the baby. She had not had any painkillers and appeared to be strongly in control of her emotions and the pain. She was peaceful and relaxed between pushing. I was in awe of the woman my daughter had become.

Elijah was water birthed at 4.30am on his due date, into the arms of his mother, without so much as a cry. It was the most amazing birth I had ever witnessed. It was a moment of pure delight and amazement. Courtney remained calm and in control, managing beautifully without pain killers of any kind. Jett seemed impressed with the birth of his son and equally in awe of the whole process of delivering a baby.

Elijah was a beautiful baby but very, very unsettled and it soon became clear that neither Courtney nor Jett were coping very well with the new addition. Courtney was plagued with feeding issues due to Elijah's inability to attach to the breast and very early on she made the painful decision to stop breastfeeding and bottle feed instead. Jett was not understanding of this and equally unable to deal with Courtney's fluctuating emotions and moments of distress as a new mother. Before too long Courtney decided that she could not cope due to Jett's lack of support and asked if we would consider letting her and the baby move back in with us.

Paul and I were reluctant to do this but felt we had no option other than to agree. Courtney had no money and no ability to earn an income. We hoped that a little bit of supported time with us might ease the situation. We went from a peaceful quiet existence to the angst-driven highs and lows of having a new mother and baby living with us who was going through a separation and trying to manage an unsettled baby.

Our lives revolved around our new baby grandson. What a precious time it was for both Paul and me. It was such a privilege for us to be ever present as our grandson grew and changed before our eyes. The baby's joy in playing with the goats and llamas, laughing at the fluffy baby doll sheep, making friends with our beautiful Cape Barren goose, Jilly; crawling around their feet and cuddling into their soft fur; rocking the baby to sleep, sitting with him whilst he played in the bath. Very precious memories.

There were still moments when Courtney had the capacity to render me senseless with her vitriolic tirades of hate and anger. The more I tried to defend myself, the more brutal the verbal assault was and I was left pondering my existence on this planet. I knew her attacks had little to do with me and everything to do with the pain she was going through at that moment in time. I was just her "safe" place, the person to whom she could unleash at, but this cycle was reaching its demise. I no longer wanted to tolerate these explosions. Something had to change because these verbal slouches effected the equilibration of my life. I needed to install some boundaries around her behaviour.

A couple of months after Courtney and Elijah moved in, Paul and I needed to take a break. We were confident leaving the animals in Courtney's care. We thought that she would enjoy a couple of weeks having the house to herself and we certainly could do with a good sleep. I'd had another major Rheumatoid arthritis flare up and this had rendered me bed prone for a number of weeks prior to the holiday.

The ten days we spent in the Cook Islands that year was one of the most memorable and relaxing holidays we'd had to date. I never remember feeling so completely at peace, so deliciously happy, so relaxed and chilled. We swam in the ocean, snorkelled for hours, rode bikes, explored on scooters, read by the pool, swung in hammocks beside the ocean. We ate at wonderful French inspired restaurants, had romantic dinners by the sea, picked up fresh fruit from the markets, bought fresh seafood from the boats. We walked, we talked, we reconnected again. It was a great holiday and we returned home completely revived.

Four days after arriving home from our holiday, just as we started to get back into the swing of life with a baby again, a cyclone called Debbie started to unexpectedly move down the coast of Queensland. Our property is situated close to the border of the state of Queensland and New South Wales, Australia. Living so far south, everyone considered the prospect of a cyclone making it to us was nearly impossible. The northern part of the state, the cyclone prone portion, is more than 1700 kilometres away.

We watched on as Cyclone Debbie was predicted to be bigger than Marcia, the category 5 system that had smashed Queensland some years earlier. Whilst Debbie did not reach this category in the end, she left a trail of destruction from northern Queensland down to northern New South Wales and continued across the ocean to New Zealand.

Phenomenal torrential rain accompanied Cyclone Debbie on her path of destruction, with up to 1000mm of rain falling in some of the areas during her reign of terror. As Cyclone Debbie was downgraded to an ex-tropical cyclone, she proceeded to continue south, dumping more rain as she went. Just off the Glitter Coast, as the weather system moved south she merged with a cold front moving up from the north coast of New South Wales, with disastrous results.

We had experienced some flooding as the system moved south and had implemented our flood plan, which consisted of moving the llamas offsite to the neighbour's property, moving the cars off-site and moving the goats to the higher ground. We anticipated about 30 centimetres of flood water across the top of the property, had prepared for this, built the house to accommodate this rare occurrence, if it were to happen.

Nothing prepared us for what eventuated that night.

At about 6pm the news had stated that the weather system was moving off-shore and that the worst of the flooding was over. We had spent the afternoon out clearing flood fences of debris from around the back of the property and had moved some equipment to higher ground. We had had some flood water over the back of the property and the gully at the front of the house had seen the flood water quite high, but nothing we hadn't seen before. The house remained high and dry. The rain had stopped and we all settled in for the night expecting some high winds.

By about 8pm Courtney and the baby were asleep, Paul was reading in the bedroom and I had a funny feeling - another one of those foreboding premonitions of something not being right. I had learnt to listen to them by now and I went to check on the water levels outside. I grabbed the big torch and walked down the back steps. What greeted me was surprising and alarming.

Where, just hours before there had been an almost empty gully, the gully was now filled with fast moving water that appeared to be rising really quickly. The rain had started to fall again, and I hurried back inside to get Paul.

We both walked outside with torches, only to be greeted by water lapping over the bank of the gully and appearing to be rising more quickly than ever. We decided that we should move the goats and sheep from the shed up onto the safety of the verandah. We got the first three goats onto the veranda and the water was lapping our ankles, by the time the next three goats were safe, it was up to our knees. The poor sheep were soaked and shocked and refusing to move out of the water. We couldn't get them up the steps. The commotion had now woken Courtney who arrived to help. The three of us struggled with the traumatised sheep, trying to lift the rain-soaked animals to safety. It was raining so hard now we could barely see in the darkness.

As the plight of the sheep became ever more desperate, we were screaming, crying and trying to lift each heavy weight onto the verandah. We were all extremely distressed, struggling to rescue the sheep and all the while the water kept rising. Finally, one big shove moved the last of the sheep up onto the verandah, just as the water started lapping at the top step of the stairs.

We were feeling quite nervous now. The water was surpassing the height that we had planned for when we built the house. We moved the goats into the laundry. By the time we had accomplished this, and locked them in with chairs to stand on, the force of the water made us flee inside the house. We could not move the sheep. We had to save ourselves. My heart lurched in pain and sadness as I suddenly realised that the poor animals had no chance of swimming to safety. The force of the water and their shocked condition made them impossible to move anywhere. We did not think the water would rise too much higher, but we were wrong.

RESILIENCE

I made the first call to the emergency services. Someone needed to know our plight and the fact that we had a nine-month old baby with us, trapped inside the house with fast rising flood water outside. The floodwater was just starting to seep into the house through the floorboards.

We closed all the doors and windows, placed towels at all the doors and moved everything we could up onto beds and furniture. The water kept rising. We let Elijah sleep blissfully in his cot until the water was lapping at his cot mattress and then moved him onto Courtney's lap as she sat on the top of the dining room table. We gathered the dogs too and all sat on the table, whilst making the second call to the emergency services. They were as worried as we were by this stage and we started to discuss the prospect of getting a helicopter to rescue the baby through the roof of the house, the problem being that it was raining so heavily now that a rescue could put more lives in danger. Our property was surrounded on all sides by large power lines, and it was pitch black outside. We lost power and lit the candles we had gathered together earlier in the evening.

The flood water was now forming small waterfalls, cascading into the house, through gaps in some of the doors. It was a very eerie feeling. Paul sat across from the dining room table on a stool, adjacent to the kitchen, and used his foot to keep the fridge, which kept floating out of its spot, at bay. As this was happening, we had a third conversation with the emergency services. We just wanted to know if the weather system was moving off the coast, because if it was, then it would stop raining and we would be safe. The phone line went dead and that was the last phone call we were able to make for about seven days.

Over the course of the next few hours we sat in silence and darkness with only a couple of candles for light. We watched as the flood water swept away our beloved goose, Jilly, our ducks and any furniture we had on the back verandah. Huge logs and debris floated past just outside the dining room window. We listened to the sound of debris as it hit the large pine tree outside the house. The noise of the flood water was ferocious, and we had to shout at times to be heard over the velocity of the rain. And still we waited.

The flood water rose much higher on the outside of the house that it did on the inside, testament to the water tight windows and doors. Had we had a watertight flooring system then perhaps we would have fared much better.

As quickly as the water rose, it suddenly subsided. It coincided with the most frightening noise we had heard during the flooding. It sounded like a helicopter landing on the roof. The whole house shuddered and shook, the noise making us all jump and fear for our lives. Initially we did think that there was a helicopter arriving to save us, but it was caused by the rapidly receding floodwater leaving the house and the steel girders and rafters under the house. It was like a huge big bath being drained of water. The floodwater was being sucked off our property and back down to the creek and out to sea. I wondered at the time if that was what a pre-tsunami sea looked and felt like.

By 2am the following morning, only six short hours after the flooding started, it was gone. With very little sleep, we tried to venture outside to assess the damage. What greeted us was beyond shocking. There was about a foot of mud covering the whole property; a big brown sludgy, smelly mess, with pockets of debris up to a metre high around the fence line. The neighbours on the high side of us walked down with a torch to see if we were okay. They brought Jilly goose with them. I was both delighted and dismayed in the same instance. It was so good to see both them and the goose, but I cried in my neighbour's arms in shock and disbelief. We did not know what to do, where to start, but most pressing was getting the baby and Courtney out of this mess and somewhere safe.

We had lost almost everything we owned. The sheep had been swept away in the floodwater, the chickens in the chicken house had all drowned, unable to make it out of their watery grave; the ducks had floated away, swept up in the currents of floodwater; the goats were up to their knees in mud and very unhappy about being locked in the laundry.

The shed, where so many of our possessions had been stored until I had time to go through them, looked like someone had gathered up all our belongings, tossed them into the air and kicked them once they had landed. We had no power, no phone, no water, everything was coated in mud, almost nothing had survived intact. Luckily for us the gas still worked, and we were able to start the day with a hot cup of tea.

Somewhere in the mess of that first day, other neighbours arrived to help, bringing a generator, pressure sprayers, squeegees, brooms and mops. I cried till I had no more tears, once again rendered numb with the shock of what we had survived, desperately unsure of how we would make it through this time. In the gloom of that first week, we started to clean up, a process that would take the next few years to complete and, in the meantime, we would make the decision to raise the house, lifting it further out of harm's way. The two metres of flood water we had had across our property would take a long time to repair.

Courtney and Elijah returned to Jett's house for a short time, more due to necessity rather than anything else. The baby needed a safe, clean home, not the muddy, grimy place that was our property at the time. As monumental as that time was for us, there were many more blessings that came from the flooding aftermath of Debbie.

The whole community banded together to help those of us that had suffered due to the unprecedented flooding. They delivered meals, hugs, flowers, replacement plants, love and companionship. I had never experienced such an outpouring of love and assistance in all my life. I cannot remember that time without thinking about the Tranquil Valley Community. Tearful thoughts of the flooding are replaced by my gratefulness and the graciousness shown to us during that period of time. I still feel that community presence today.

The community encouraged us with their words of kindness, empowered us to keep going and lifted us up when we could not go on anymore. We had neighbours take the dogs, wash them and look after them for weeks; we had people pick up the goats and take them to safety and love them like we did; we had strangers drop off money; we had people, including school friends I hadn't seen in 30 years, drop in and help remove debris from our property; a local earthmoving business provided us with a huge load of gravel to assist with the "mud" problem on the property; we had people mow for us whilst our tractor mower was being repaired.

For all the trauma I had suffered in my life this one was the most empowering. What a privilege and a blessing to experience the love and outpouring of tenderness we received from everyone during that time.

With the flood, there seemed to be a metaphoric cleansing of our lives. So many of the cherished "things" we had kept as mementos of life were gone. The cleansing of the flood seemed to purge my life of all the bad, like the bad had been swept away with the receding floodwater. It restored my faith in humanity, caused me to start to think outside myself and changed the way I saw life.

Lives matter more than possessions and losing so much brought into sharp focus the things that matter; the safety of loved ones; time with people who genuinely care about you; the concept that you really don't need so many material "things" to feel and understand happiness.

The dismay at the loss of so many of our carefully cultivated plants and trees was replaced by the joy of seeing just what trees can and do survive and the wonder of seeing my roses bloom for the first time after the flood, full of debris, devoid of foliage but flowering nonetheless.

We had complete, comprehensive rural insurance, but strangely enough, the insurance process was more traumatising than the actual event. To get the insurance company to pay and assist us in the recovery and rectification of our home, we had to escalate our claim to the Federal government level. It was a month before we even had an insurance assessor visit us and by then we had managed to clean the shed so that we could live temporarily in there, whilst the inside of the house was cleaned, quarantined, repaired and rebuilt.

We were able to obtain a temporary transportable shower and toilet, together with a couple of demountable buildings so that Courtney and the baby could return to live with us on the property and we had somewhere to safely cook and eat, that wasn't dirty with the filth of the flood. Both Paul and I continued to work whilst battling with the insurance company to pay for and commence works. It took ten months for us to move back into our home. Luckily it was repaired to new, we had a revamped kitchen and bathroom and a much higher house, hopefully well out of floodwater.

Courtney really battled in the fallout from the flood. She had lost all her belongings, as they too, were stored in the shed. She struggled with the breakdown of her relationship and being a new mum and she continued to aim her pain at me. I tried to be patient but was increasingly exhausted from the trauma of the flood and the flare ups of my Rheumatoid Arthritis. I knew she was struggling, but this time so were Paul and I. The impact of the flood on Paul was quite evident. He was angry and grumpy, exhausted from the constant struggle to work long hours, five days a week at his job and then the two full days over the weekend to clean-up and repair after the flood.

All the tension, angst and pain finally came to a head on an explosive afternoon when Paul decided that Courtney's treatment of me was more than enough. Courtney had unleashed on me when I had not done something she thought I should have done with the baby. Perhaps I had rocked him to sleep when I should have just put him down to settle himself off to sleep. I cannot remember the specifics, but certainly it was not issue enough for her to unleash her vile hatred towards me that afternoon.

Paul listened for a while and then said that we'd had enough and if

Courtney was not going to appreciate all that we did for her and had provided for her, and start treating her mother with some respect, then she could go and find a place of her own to live where she had to pay rent, pay for groceries and electricity and see what real life was like as an adult.

The recriminations from Courtney that afternoon were horrendous; she blamed me for all that was wrong in her life, all her misery and the fact that now my husband was kicking her out too. I felt incredibly torn by our deteriorating relationship, happening before my eyes, again. We had worked so hard to repair it and now it seemed to be falling apart again. I searched her eyes to see if there was any insight into her own behaviour, or an understanding of what we were providing. There was none. In that moment, I realised that I had to let her go; had to let her discover life on her own terms.

In two short weeks, Courtney packed up her meagre belongings and with the money we had given her from the proceeds of the insurance payout on our furniture loss, set up her first flat on the northern Glitter Coast. She was now living 45 minutes from us. I missed the grandbaby so much, it was a wrench to not have him with us all the time, to not see him every day and spend time playing and enjoying his baby gorgeousness. I did feel relieved to not have to deal with Courtney's moods or her angry outbursts anymore, though.

Courtney and Elijah thrived once they settled into their flat. Courtney's new-found independence was enriching for her and her acknowledgement that she still had to work on her own problems caused our relationship to finally start healing in a meaningful and mature way. She grabbed onto her healing with both hands and sought to learn and improve her reactions to life, and her knowledge of herself tenfold. As her mother it was wonderful to see these changes in her. There would be one final hurdle to jump though.

After six months of living in a flat in suburbia, Courtney decided that she and Elijah would like to live out in the countryside again. She searched until she found a share home for the two of them to move into. Once we had her settled again, she had her first interstate trip away to meet up with a girlfriend. Jett was taking Elijah for the weekend and Courtney was excited to be having a little time to herself. We enjoyed a rare lunch together on the way to the airport.

I offered to drop her off and pick her up from the airport, negating the cost of airport parking. I picked her up from the airport in her car on the Sunday after her visit and on the trip home we had one of the worst arguments we had ever had. Once more she was personally attacking me for the misery she perceived her life to be, from being a single parent, to the lack of a decent man in her life, to the health issues she battled and the anxiety she felt. Each time I tried to defend myself she unleashed more and more verbal abuse. By the time she dropped me off to my car and Paul, I was shocked and in tears. Once more I felt like I could not go on, that I was responsible for all that was wrong in her life. Paul calmed me down, but as we set off on our afternoon of paddling, the tears started to flow. The realisation that I could not tolerate any more verbal abuse in my life hit me like a physical slap in the face and with each stroke of the paddle in the water my mind started to think and develop a rational plan to protect myself in the future. I knew that her abuse stemmed from a fear and pain that overtook any rational thought she had at the time, but I also knew that she was in a place where she had the power to stop herself attacking the one person who had always stood steadfastly by her side.

As we pulled the kayaks into shore, I started to talk to Paul about what the future for Courtney and I held. I grappled with the thought that I could not completely cut her out of my life, could not imagine life without her and Elijah in it, but it had gotten to the place where I needed to start to protect my own sanity from her onslaughts. I knew it would be days before she contacted me again and by then the sting of her words would be lessened and I could talk to her in a calm manner.

It was three days before I heard from Courtney and her text message belayed none of the angst from the weekend. No apology, no recognition of what had transpired between us. I told her I would call her later in the day to talk as I had something to discuss with her.

I called as Courtney finished work for the day and got straight into the conversation that we had needed to have for many, many years. I explained how hurt and disillusioned I was by her attack on the weekend and as usual she defended her position. This time I just listened until she was done talking and simply stated the following. That from this point on, I would no longer accept her verbal attacks on me and I intended to walk away from her if she did it in person, hang up the phone if she did it over the phone and if it happened in the car again, I would remove myself from the car immediately. I needed to clearly articulate the new boundaries I had put in place round me and I needed her to understand that this was a line in the sand that she could no longer cross. The time had come to control her emotions, sit with and deal with the pain she felt in that moment and move on without attacking me anymore. It was the first time I was conscious of her understanding and ability to comply. It had been relatively simple and relatively painless. I also left me with a feeling of peaceful resignation.

After this conversation, life once again settled into a routine of flood rectification, replanting of trees and shrubs, and cleaning, so much cleaning. Over the course of the next eighteen months we slowly returned our property to some sort of normality. Slowly we all began to enjoy life again.

Since that time Courtney and Elijah have settled into a routine of part time work/day-care and shared custody arrangements with Jett. She has yet to find a relationship that works for her. Billy has started his

Doctorate of Physiotherapy and is excelling in his studies. He and his partner are planning more overseas holidays.

I have reflected on what we have all been through, all that we have achieved and some of the things I have learnt.

I found reconnection with some of the people from my past has been incredibly healing for me. I reconnected with Andrew, his family, his parents and became good friends with his younger sister. I've spent quality time reconnecting with people from school and nursing and this has brought balance, hope, support and encouragement into my life. I've found new and beautiful friendships and enjoy what these relationships bring to my life. Daniel (my first husband) and I have a good friendship now and he even helped out after the flood.

I also discovered that I needed to put boundaries around members of my family to protect myself and encourage the continued healing of my mind. This strategy combined with forgiveness has assisted my overall resilience and return to general health. I love my parents and my siblings, but I now also love and value myself in that equation.

My battle with Rheumatoid Arthritis is ongoing but has been stable and well managed for the last twelve months.

Finally, the powers of a committed, loving partnership in life cannot be underestimated. My husband has been the most calming, rational, loving presence in my life. His steadying influence and quiet support has enabled me to thrive and strive to be better. He has my back and I love him absolutely.

As I finish this book, I am sitting on the back verandah, watching the llamas and goats graze in the beautiful late evening glow that accompanies the approaching darkness and pondering life. I look to the mountains beyond our farm, over the creek and beyond our pastures, I think about life resilience. I no longer wonder "what will go wrong next" or "what will happen next". I know that no matter what life has to throw at me, it is all going to be fine. I feel an overwhelming sense of peace and peacefulness, a deep happiness and contentedness. I realise in this moment that I have discovered my own personal resilience. A resilience to life, a resilience to trauma, an ability to rebuild myself and not play the same records in my mind. I have discovered the secret to true, deep and abiding happiness. I am satisfied, life is amazingly good!

I smile to myself, breathe in the purified valley air and let the contented happiness seep through my body, enjoying the moment and smiling at the gloriousness of life.

TONI LONTIS

Epilogue

"Forgiveness is giving up the hope that the past could have been any different." OPRAH WINFREY

It's important in this part of the book to include information on the type of trauma that Courtney suffered and what she has dealt with and will deal with for the rest of her life. It is important to protect and nurture someone so irrevocably damaged.

According to Janoff-Bulman, trauma shatters three central assumptions that we have of the world: "the belief in personal invulnerability, the perception of the world as a meaningful place and the perception of oneself as positive." With that mind I want to briefly discuss the immediate and long-term effects of childhood sexual abuse as they relate specifically to Courtney.

Young girls who are the victims of sexual abuse experience physical, biological and behavioural problems that can persist for decades after the assaults.

Victims are at a greater risk for the following:

- Musculoskeletal pain symptoms including headaches (J. Leserman et El 1998)

- Back aches (Irish et El 2009);

- Muscle aches (Newman et al., 2000)

- Fibromyalgia (Walker et al., 1997)

- Joint pain (Walker, et al., 1999);

- General pain symptoms (Golding, 1994; Raphaeel 2001);

- Increased risk of psychopathology, especially post-traumatic stress disorder (PTSD), depression, and substance abuse (Browne & Finkelhor, 1986), as well as increased depression, anxiety disorders, antisocial behaviour, substance abuse, eating disorders, and suicidal behaviour. (Zlotnick et el., 1996) (Wilsnack et el 1997) (Thakka et el 2000)

- Fundamental damage is inflicted on the child's developing capacities for trust, intimacy, agency and sexuality, and many other mental health problems of adult life can be associated with histories of abuse. (Shonkoff 2009)

- Future victimisation regardless of age, educational attainment, employment status, income or marital status. Again, re-victimisation is not inevitable

- Distorted self-perception - survivors often develop a belief that they caused the sexual abuse and that they deserved it. These beliefs may result in self-destructive relationships.

- Disturbances of desire, arousal, and orgasm may result from the association between sexual activity, violation, and pain. Survivors are more likely to have had 50 or more intercourse partners, have had a sexually transmitted infection and engage in risk-taking behaviors that place them at risk of contracting human immunodeficiency virus

- Gynecologic problems, including chronic pelvic pain, dyspareunia, vaginismus, and nonspecific vaginitis, are common diagnoses among survivors

- May be less skilled at self-protection. They are more apt to accept being victimised by others.
This tendency to be victimised repeatedly may be the result of general vulnerability in dangerous situations and exploitation by untrustworthy people.

- Harms a child's lifelong ability to establish trusting, intimate relationships (Springer et el 2003)

- Experiencing incest, or carnal knowledge as a minor, can lead to a traumatic bonding, a form of relatedness in which the perpetrator mistreats the other with abuse, threats, intimidation, beatings, humiliations and harassment, but it also provides the victim with attention, some form of affection and connectedness. It is a seriously diabolical crime!

The process by which a perpetrator stages their crime is also an important consideration in Courtney's story.

Sgroi and colleagues have described a 5-stage process in the sexual mistreatment of children, commonly known as Grooming.

GROOMING

STAGE 1. ENGAGEMENT

The child/teenager is brought into a closer relationship with the perpetrator. He or she becomes involved in more intense and gradually sexualised behaviours via special attention that engages the child/teenager's emotional needs en route to sexual behaviours that may be normalised and introduced gradually as games or as activities that clearly bring the child the desired attention. Some perpetrators use violence or threats to co-erce sexual engagement.

Stage 2. The sexual interaction phase,

The perpetrator builds on the preliminary grooming of the victim, and the initial sexual involvements escalate, often progressing from exposure and touching to the penetration of one or more orifices.

STAGE 3. SECRECY

Efforts are made to ensure privacy, to reduce the victim's understanding of the abuser's accountability, and to set the stage for ongoing sexual activity. The child/teenager is made to feel responsible and to understand that revelation would have very bad consequences. This "understanding" involves threats of harm to the child or others. Threats include loss of attachment (because the child will be seen as bad by others or would lose the affection of the perpetrator and others); being told that the child would not be believed; being assured that the child really wanted what was done; being told the child will be rejected by God for not honouring his father, stepfather etc. The child often emerges from this brainwashing with profound self-loathing, convinced that he or she is evil and that any revelation would only confirm his or her badness and guarantee rejection.

STAGE 4. DISCLOSURE

The secret gets out, either spontaneously, accidentally or deliberately. The reaction of concerned others is more likely to be determined by the perpetrator's role in the family, family loyalty, and shame than by the best interests of the child. Families tend to be most protective of the child when the perpetrator is not a parent or a sibling. Not uncommonly, the family becomes protective and defensive in its anxiety and moves to disavow the severity of the offence and its sequels and to blame the victim and any authorities or professionals who become involved.

STAGE 5. SUPPRESSION

The community of concerned individuals within and associated with the family moves to suppress the veracity of the child's report, minimizing both the severity of the mistreatment and its consequences. The group does not want to deal with the consequences of the ugly truth and are eager to avoid the shame and inconvenience of dealing with agencies and professionals. Individuals may actively try to discredit the child or pressure him to recant accusations.

Only a small proportion of childhood sexual assault cases will ever result in prosecution. This has been blamed, at least on structures within law that continue to prejudice the outcomes of sexual offence cases (Mack 1998) I can also reflect that there appears to be a systemic prejudice that 'woman and children' especially girl-children possess a seemingly natural propensity to lie about sexual abuse and to fabricate allegations (Taylor 2004:5) This reflection is one that makes me angry, especially on the behalf of my daughter. Bearing all this in mind, the fact that we got a conviction should have been encouraging, but once Aamon was released from jail all that encouragement was lost and Courtney was destroyed once more.

Luckily, Courtney had changed her name, changed phone numbers and moved addresses by the time Aamon was released from jail. This does not stop him from trying to contact her every couple of years or so. We have been able to thwart these attempts before he actually got to her. They have consisted of friend requests on Facebook, LinkedIn messages and messages from secondary people. The whole family actively manages their privacy settings on all social media to prevent this and we all have unlisted private phone numbers. None of us has run into Aamon in person and that is probably for the best.

Courtney had and will suffer from many of the symptoms I have described, and her journey is obviously similar to so many others out there. She will need lifelong psychological care and I worry about the impacts of these crimes on her physical health in years to come. She is doing as best she can with life and her baby son gives her a happiness and purpose for living.

I'm grateful she is still here to enjoy life, whatever that looks like for her.

> "It's your reaction to adversity, not adversity itself that determines how your life's story will develop." DIETER F. UCHTDORF

TONI LONTIS

About the author

Toni lives on a small acreage property in the hinterland adjacent to the pristine beaches of Queensland's Gold Coast, Australia. She lives with her husband and an assortment of dogs, goats, llamas, ducks and chickens and enjoys long visits from her two adult children, their partners and her grandson.

Toni is a nurse who formerly worked as a nurse consultant in her own company, before retiring to pursue her dream of writing a book or three.

Toni grew up on a rural property in the middle of nowhere. After completing her nursing training at a general hospital, in regional Queensland, she spent the next 30 years working as a nurse in a variety of roles from clinical nursing to management, culminating with the formation of her own company in 2012. As a nurse consultant for her company, she provided safety and quality support to small hospitals across the country. Her work involved process management, clinical management and lots of health-based writing.

Her creative writing journey did not commence until 2018 with her first book, Resilience, a memoir that details her struggle with depression, anxiety and trauma in her life and how she overcame this to lead a healthy, happy, fulfilling life. She is passionate about self-awareness, self-improvement and being the best person she can be.

Her upcoming second book 'Whole Again' details the strategies she used to ensure her own healing and personal growth. Her deep desire is to inspire other people with her story of struggle and overcoming trauma. Telling her unique story sees Toni speaking around the country and overseas.

When she's not writing you can find her talking to her beloved goats, laughing with her husband or enjoying time with her wee grandson. An avid gardener and small farm hobbyist, she also wants to write about the joys of owning goats and small-scale hobby farm self-sustainability.

A writer by day and an avid Facebook scanner by night, she is loath to discuss herself in the third person but can be persuaded to do so from time to time.

You can find her on:

- Facebook
https://www.facebook.com/groups/1288997961190724/ -Everyday Women's Business

- www.everydaywomensbusiness.com.au

- www.resiliencebook.com.au

- www.tonilontis.com.au

TONI LONTIS

Acknowledgements

My Husband – my amazingly supportive empowering husband, I could not have done this without you.

My Son – my gorgeous, talented photographer, physiotherapist son. Thank you for being you. I love you more than words can express.

Editor- to the wonderful Sarah, who challenged me and encouraged me each step of the way thank you.

Fiona – thank you for the name of this book and your ongoing friendship - it is precious to me.

Michelle – for all your encouragement, support, acknowledgement and understanding. My words cannot convey the depth of gratitude I feel towards you.

Family and friends – to my amazing tribe, family and friends. Where would I be without each and every one of you? Thank you for your unending support.

Nat and Stuart – No words could cover the depth of gratitude I feel towards the two of you, for your program, your teachings, your support, your belief. Thank you.

Hotlines to help

- 1800 Respect national helpline 1800 737 732

- Women's Crisis Line 1800 811 811

- Men's Referral Service 1300 766 491

- Lifeline (24 hour crisis line) 131 114

- Relationships Australia 1300 364 277

- Kids Helpline 1800 55 1800

References

Brown J, Berenson K, Cohen P. Documented and self-reported child abuse and adult pain in a community sample. Clinical Journal of Pain. 2005;21:374–377

Domino JV, Haber JD. Prior physical and sexual abuse in women with chronic headache: Clinical correlates. Headache. 1987;27:310–314

Golding JM, Cooper LM, George LK. Sexual assault history and health perceptions: Seven general population studies. Health Psychology. 1997;16:417–425.

Judith Lewis Herman. Trauma and Recovery : The Aftermath of Violence--From Domestic Abuse to Political Terror Published May 30th 1997 by Basic Books

Irish, Leah & Kobayashi, Ihori & L Delahanty, Douglas. (2009). Journal of Pediatric Psychology 35(5):450-61 · December 2009 Long-term Physical Health Consequences of Childhood

Janoff-Bulman,R (1992) Shattered Assumtions:Towards a new psychology of Trauma. NEW YORK, NY Free Press

Leserman, J, Z. LI , D. A. DROSSMAN and Y. J. B. HU

Psychological Medicine Volume 28, Issue 2 March 1998, pp. 417-425 Selected symptoms associated with sexual and physical abuse history among female patients with gastrointestinal disorders: the impact on subsequent health care visits

Mack, K. (1998), "You should scrutinise her evidence with great care': Corroboration of women's testimony about sexual assault', in P. Easteal (ed.), Balancing the Scales: Rape, Law Reform and Australian Culture, The Federation Press, Sydney

Raphael KG, Widom CS, Lange G. Childhood victimization and pain in adulthood: A prospective investigation. Pain. 2001;92:283–293.

Sgroi SM, Blick LC, Porter FS. A conceptual framework for child sexual abuse. In: Sgroi SM, ed. Handbook of Clinical Intervention in Child Sexual Abuse. Lexington, MA: Lexington Books; 1982:9-37.

Shonkoff JP, Boyce WT, McEwen BS. Neuroscience, molecular biology, and the childhood roots of health disparities. Building a new framework for health promotion and disease prevention. Journal of the American Medical Association. 2009;301:2252–2259

Springer KW, Sheridan J, Kuo D, Carnes M. The long-term health outcomes of childhood abuse. An overview and a call to action. Journal of General Internal Medicine. 2003;18:864–870

Taylor, S. C. (2004), Surviving the legal system, Coulomb Communications, Melbourne.

Thakkar RR, McCanne TR. The effects of daily stressors on physical health in women with and without a childhood history of sexual abuse. Child Abuse & Neglect. 2000;24:209–221

Walker EA, Keegan D, Gardner G, Sullivan M, Bernstein D, Katon WJ. Psychosocial factors in fibromyalgia compared with rheumatoid arthritis: II. Sexual, physical, and emotional abuse and neglect. Psychosomatic Medicine. 1997;59:572–577.

Wilsnack SC, Vogeltanz ND, Klassen AD, Harris TR. Childhood sexual abuse and women's substance abuse: National survey findings. Journal of Studies on Alcohol. 1997;58:264–271.

Zlotnick C, Zakriski AL, Shea MT, Costello E, Begin A, Pearlstein T, et al. The long-term sequalae of sexual abuse: Support for a complex posttraumatic stress disorder. Journal of Traumatic Stress. 1996;9:195–205.

http://www.kbsolutions.com/Grooming.pdf

"Under His Spell": Victims' Perspectives of being Groomed Online Helen C. Whittle 1,2,*, Catherine E. Hamilton-Giachritsis 2 and Anthony R. Beech 2 social sciences ISSN 2076-0760 www.mdpi.

com/journal/socsci

http://www.oprah.com/oprahshow/child-sexual-abuse-6-stages-of-grooming/all

http://www.psychiatrictimes.com/sexual-offenses/ramifications-incest

RESILIENCE

TONI LONTIS

www.ingramcontent.com/pod-product-compliance
Lightning Source LLC
Chambersburg PA
CBHW021056080526
44587CB00010B/270